HOPE
BEYOND REASON

HOPE

BEYOND REASON

EMBRACED BY GOD'S PRESENCE
IN THE TOUGHEST OF TIMES

DAVE HESS

DESTINY IMAGE® PUBLISHERS, INC.

P.O. Box 310, Shippensburg, PA 17257-0310

"Speaking to the Purposes of God for this Generation and for the Generations to Come."

This book and all other Destiny Image, Revival Press, Mercy Place, Fresh Bread, Destiny Image Fiction, and Treasure House books are available at Christian bookstores and distributors worldwide.

For a U.S. bookstore nearest you, call 1-800-722-6774.
For more information on foreign distributors, call 717-532-3040.
Reach us on the Internet at www.destinyimage.com.

ISBN 10: 0-7684-2697-9
ISBN 13: 978-0-7684-2697-7

For Worldwide Distribution, Printed in the U.S.A.
2 3 4 5 6 7 8 9 10 11 / 12 11 10 09 08

To Sheri

You are a precious gift,
devoting your heart to beat
with mine for a lifetime.

What a joy this journey has been!

Even in the hardest of times, you stood with me.
You prayed and fought for my life.

You loved and you served.
Tirelessly. Resolutely.

Without a complaint.

I have seen the face of love.
I wake up to it each morning.

Acknowledgments

My heart is filled with gratitude for so many wonderful people who have touched my life with Jesus' love. Many of them are mentioned in the pages of this book.

I want to honor those who have helped to make the writing of this story a reality:

Thom Gardner—Good friend, author, coach, and encourager. You lit a fire in my spirit. You fanned the flames of that fire. Then you held my feet to that same fire until I crawled my way to the laptop. I appreciate you!

Elise Jackson—With your red pen and your amazing gift with words, you inspired me. I look forward to the day when your heart touches the hearts of many through the pages of your books.

Todra Payne—Thank you for your insights, straightforward critiques, and tons of encouragement!

Debra Benedict—Your prayers, your promptings, and your passion for correct grammar are hugely appreciated!

Tim Spirk—You gave much time and energy to help me put my heart on a page.

Tom and Heidi Ryan—What a creative team you are! Your ability to communicate the Father's heart is exhilarating!

Parke and Betsy Adams—You spent most of your vacation refining the final edit!?! My gratitude for you goes beyond words.

Karen Gierhart—Details, details, details! You are an amazing assistant, servant of the Lord, and friend. Sheri and I think the world of you!

Endorsements

For years I've been telling the miraculous testimony of Dave Hess. There are so many lessons in his story. In one sense it is a life-changing account of how one man beat death because he did not stand alone. In another sense it illustrates the quality of faith, tenacity, and humility needed to wrestle with God and circumstances until breakthrough comes. To the scientific community Dave Hess is a walking medical miracle; to a fellow believer he is an inspirational model of the kind of man who cannot die until his life purpose is complete. I'm thrilled to see this story finally being put into print.

Dr. Lance Wallnau
Apostolic Overseer, Word of Life Covenant Church
Lance Wallnau Ministries

My friend Dave Hess has written an exceptional book that will build your faith: his own miraculous story sharing the process of his healing from leukemia. This incredible book will build your faith and prepare you to experience miracles as normal Christianity. The book you are holding in your hand is not about theory. I smiled and wept through this remarkable book as Dave's humanity, transparency, and faith come through each page. It will inspire you to new heights of faith and compassion as you experience God in a new way. I highly recommend this book.

Larry Kreider, author and speaker
Author of *House to House* and
Authentic Spiritual Mentoring
International Director,
DOVE Christian Fellowship International

Dave Hess is a great storyteller. His warm heart and down-to-earth humor make you feel like you've known him for years. This story is true, intensely personal, and full of spiritual insights. We couldn't stop turning the pages, laughing and crying as we read the story of his miraculous healing from leukemia.

Charles and Anne Stock
Senior Pastors, Life Center Ministries

Dave Hess has written an amazing autobiography that will connect you with the realities of God's love and healing power. His story will increase your faith and expand your expectations for miracles. His testimony, along with ever-increasing accounts all across the globe, are living proof that nothing is impossible with God. The realities of His Kingdom are within our grasp right now.

Dr. Che Ahn
Author of *How to Pray for Healing* and
Close Encounters of the Divine Kind
President, Harvest International Ministry

Hope Beyond Reason is one of the best-written books I have read in my entire life. It reads like a novel, but it's the true story of a man who was given a death sentence by his doctor, and yet many years later he lives on to chronicle his life's miracle. This is much more than a testimonial book; this is an epic classic, a journey from the edge of death to the gates of glory! If you have ever found yourself in an impossible situation, drowning in the quicksand of hopeless despair or lost in the valley of darkness, this book is for you. *Hope Beyond Reason* is your knight in shining armor, the light in a dark tunnel, and a rescue rope to those who are going down for the last time. This is a must read for everyone in need of a miracle!

Kris Vallotton
Author of *The Supernatural Ways of Royalty*
and *Developing a Supernatural Lifestyle*
Founder of the Bethel School of Supernatural Ministry
Senior Associate Leader of Bethel Church
Redding, California

In Dave's inimitable communication style, he blends heart, humor, and hope. Dave's drama of healing involves a cast of characters from family, friends, congregation, and Heaven. Scripture passages are the heroes in this journal of faith. They serve as anchors of hope and the sails of wisdom for a pastor navigating the storm of suffering and ministering from a hospital bed.

Keith E. Yoder
Author of *Healthy Leaders*
Founder and President, Teaching the Word Ministries

This book will make you cry, laugh, and then reflect on the greatness of God. When you or a loved one faces cancer, you need hope and reality walking together. This book helps you keep a balanced earthly and heavenly perspective. An easy, stimulating read that blessed me.

Rachel Hickson
Author of *Supernatural Communication*
and Little Keys Open Big Doors
Founder, Heartcry for Change

Table of Contents

Foreword

Dave Hess's new book brought me to tears more than once as I read a very real and emotional story of his fight with leukemia. The first time I met Dave, he was in the hospital in a desperate fight for his life. (I will let Dave tell that story.) Later, after moving to the Harrisburg area, I began to attend Christ Community Church, and I sat under his teaching for a few years. He is one of the very best teachers I have ever heard. He has a compassionate pastor's heart. Dave has done the Church a service in writing about his battle with cancer. It is a testimony to the faithfulness of God and to the Hess family's faith. It reveals how to stand in faith, prayer, hope, and love in the midst of life's greatest battle—the battle against death.

The book is riveting. I found myself reading it until 4:30 in the morning, until I couldn't stay awake anymore. I had almost finished it in one reading. When I woke up I grabbed the book again to finish the story. I believe there is a powerful message in the book for anyone struggling with any life-threatening disease.

Hope Beyond Reason is also the story of how God worked a tremendous miracle in what seemed a certain death sentence. No wonder Pastor Dave Hess has such a hunger to see the large church he pastors become a center for healing. What God did to spare Dave's life is, without any doubt, a great miracle. This book, however, is not just about a man with great faith in a great God, but it is also the story of a great church that believed in, prayed for, fought for, and loved their pastor through his battle with death.

I am glad to have Dave Hess as a friend, fellow crusader for the ministry of healing, my former pastor, and now a published author. He has done a great job in pointing people to God in the midst of the crisis of life. As any family shocked by the discovery that one of its members is ill, this story is not just about Dave, it is also his family's story. The family's insights during the battle and their report of the victory brought me to tears.

During the years I listened to Dave preach, he mentioned a few times about his battle with cancer. As a friend, he shared with me briefly about his battle. The drama of the battle needed to be written. Only in the full story does one fully comprehend the power of faith and love to move the mountains of problems in our lives.

Thanks, Dave, for being such a great storyteller.

Hope Beyond Reason is not a self-help book based upon discovering the right "principles" to give you victory. Instead, it is a book about the importance of discovering the "Prince of Peace" who can give you the victory. It glorifies the intimate role of the *paracletos*—the Holy Spirit

(translated in John 14 as comforter, counselor, helper)—
and His wonderful gift of healing. *Hope Beyond Reason* is
about the Healer as much as it is about the healed.

Randy Clark
Global Awakening Apostolic Missions Network
Author of *There Is More, Lighting Fires*
and *God Can Use Little Ole Me*
Mechanicsburg, Pennsylvania

Introduction

I wrote this book for you. To encourage you.

Because life can be difficult. Seemingly impossible at times.

Some days I've wished that life would be like a movie. In most films when something bad is about to happen, the music changes—a minor key, heavy bass, and screeching violins signal danger is right around the corner. But life isn't like that. Often things seem to hit us without warning.

That was the case for my family and me a few short years ago. In a moment, our world seemed to fall apart. Our daily routines and long-term dreams were put on hold as we faced the sobering realities of life and death. In fact, a lot of reality hit us all at once!

In the middle of all this "reality," we searched for the truth.

And we found Him.

We discovered Jesus Christ to be true to His word. True to every promise He had ever made. True to His nature. And truly, the Lover of our souls.

We came into deeper places of knowing Him to be a wonderful counselor to our weary hearts. We drew near to Him as our shelter in the fiercest of storms. Like a good shepherd guarding his sheep, He led us through dark and dangerous passageways. He kept us from falling. He kept us from falling apart. He healed us. He lifted us out of despair.

He opened a door of hope for us and then led us through it. He gave us a peace beyond our imagination. And a hope beyond reason.

And He's holding the door for you!

Chapter 1

A Journey of Faith Begins

He will have no fear of bad news;
his heart is steadfast, trusting in the Lord.
...In the end he will look in triumph on his foes
(Psalm 112:7-8).

The phone call shattered the silence of that late November evening. Though it was the Monday of Thanksgiving week in 1997, I felt anything but festive. I lumbered across the kitchen floor in fierce competition with the answering machine. Snagging the handset moments before the "We're not home right now..." message, I grinned at my minor victory in the never-ending battle of "Man vs. Machine."

The woman's voice on the other end was firm. And frustrated.

"Mr. Hess, where have you been?" she questioned, her irritation enunciating every word. "We have been trying to reach you all afternoon! *Where* have you been?" she repeated indignantly.

I apologized for not checking our answering machine and imagined a sly grin coming from the digital device in the next room (score: Man—1; Machine—1).

"We have the results of your blood test," she continued. "It is urgent that you come to our office as soon as possible." The seriousness of her tone began to unsettle me.

"I'll be right there," I responded abruptly. Grabbing my keys while trying to force my foot into a shoe, I began to wonder what the "urgent" part was. The tests were taken just a few hours ago. *Couldn't this wait until morning?*

It was Monday, our day to tie up loose ends before another week was off and running ahead of us. Grocery shopping, house cleaning, banking, and "other duties as assigned" made up our typical Mondays together. But this Monday was anything but typical. My wife Sheri was running a few errands, trying to make up for the time we lost sitting in hospital waiting rooms throughout the day.

I quickly told our 16-year-old daughter Bethany that she was in charge of her younger brothers, Ben (age 12) and Brandon (age 9)—a role she enjoyed maybe a little too much. I overheard her barking a few orders to the boys as I staggered into the garage. While my mind was swimming with thoughts, my body was void of energy. Gingerly I backed the car onto the driveway. Within moments I was on the road, heading into one of the fiercest storms of my life.

For several months leading up to this Monday, I had been battling fatigue and what appeared to be flu symptoms. Yet other strange things were happening to me. One day after sitting in a wooden chair with lattice designs, I noticed those same patterns etched in bruises on my back. Black and blue patches were also appearing on my arms and legs. A strange brownish hue discolored the whites of my eyes. It seemed as if each day greeted me with a new disfigurement.

I was also experiencing constant bleeding around my teeth and gums. I discovered it one Saturday on my way to the grocery store. Looking into the car's rearview mirror, I was shocked to see my bright red smile. After quickly wiping my teeth, I dashed into the store to make a few fast purchases before returning home. As I smiled at the cashier on my way out, her startled look halted me. "Your teeth are bleeding," she said, pointing at my mouth. Wanting to calm her fears (and mine), I dryly joked that I had been sampling beef roasts in the meat department. Why I said that and where it came from, I do not know. The poor clerk only looked more puzzled.

And I was, too.

What was happening to my body?

I was tired. Very tired. Besides the appearance of strange bruises, a hazy cloud hovered in my mind. I felt dull and detached from people and the events happening around me. Like a prisoner in my own body, I was watching life go by from a distant observation room. And I could not escape.

I blamed my bleeding gums on irregular flossing habits, imagining my dentist's frown as he detailed the merits of dragging a string through my molars. The rest of the symptoms were beginning to scare me. I knew something was wrong with me—something serious.

The morning after the ghastly grocery visit was the Sunday before Thanksgiving. As pastor of a local church near Harrisburg, Pennsylvania, I loved gathering each week with our dear friends. Encouraging them with the words of the Lord was one of my greatest joys. In spite of my physical weakness, I gradually awoke that Sunday morning, eager to share my heart with those we love.

We had moved to the Harrisburg area in 1989 just to be part of this church. As young Messiah College students in the early 1970s, Sheri and I were deeply affected by a nearby church called Bethany Tabernacle. Despite our rather subdued religious upbringing, we connected with these people who were warm, friendly, and lively. Overcoming our culture shock, we fell right in with this group of crazy, committed followers of Jesus. And the connection lasted.

I became the third pastor of this great church. The two previous leaders, Russell Tiday and Larry Titus, are wonderful godly men. They laid a strong foundation from which we are still reaping the results of their labors of love.

I learned so many things from Pastor Russell during my college years. I discovered that Jesus Christ was a friend whom I could know and talk to. I came to follow Jesus as the ultimate leader of my life and to experience deeper dimensions of His love for me. I also saw Jesus' power at work—healing and restoring people just like He did when He walked the earth. Russell taught me to believe that Jesus could do the same thing in me.

As newlyweds, Sheri and I had agreed to pastor two rural churches. Sheri worked at a local bookstore, while I was a full-time seminary student. The combination of long hours and little experience eventually took its toll on us and on the churches. After a painful church split, they looked for another pastor. I searched for another career.

When I met Larry Titus, I was a disillusioned former pastor, now working in the administration of a nursing home. Grateful to find employment, Sheri and I adjusted to the change in our lifestyle. The residents at the center became like a second family to me. The hours were wonderful. I was home with my family every night. Our weekends were free from church responsibilities. I began enjoying the fact that being a pastor was part of my former life. At least I thought I was enjoying it, but persistent stirrings in my heart told me I longed to return and do what I was created to do.

At the prompting of my wife, I called Pastor Larry to receive his counsel. To my surprise, he offered me a job as a staff pastor at the church. I thought I needed counseling; and he wanted to hire me! I was trying hard to convince him that I was a mess, but he saw beyond my disillusionment and spoke to my heart. Larry believed in me when I was struggling to believe in myself.

So there I was, on a Sunday morning of Thanksgiving week, waking up to another opportunity to encourage people to believe.

Sheri's voice seemed miles away as she called me back to consciousness. Slithering from my bed, I groggily washed, dressed, blotted my teeth, and walked out the door. The bleeding from my mouth was more profuse that morning, so I took a few extra handkerchiefs along just in case.

The message stirring in my heart that day was from Hebrews 11. Some call it the "faith chapter."

Through a haze of weariness, I shared my heart. "Faith is a gift from God," I declared. "With it, He enables us to believe His promises…even when we cannot see His fulfillment of them." Mopping the blood from my mouth, I continued, "He strengthens us to have confidence in Him when confusion is all around us. In the middle of a life-threatening storm, faith is our Father holding our lives in His firm hands and softly pleading, 'Trust Me!'"

These are the words I shared in my sermon that Sunday morning in November of 1997. Little did I know how crucial their truth would be in the journey that was about to begin. I would learn how sturdy and powerful His gift of faith really is.

The rest of that Sunday was a blur, most of it lost to sleep.

By Monday, I felt significantly worse. Overnight my tongue became covered with black sores, which extended throughout the inside of my mouth. Sheri took one look at me and said, "That's it. I'm calling the doctor!" To her surprise, I immediately agreed. Normally, I avoid doctors, as they have a tendency to either inject something into you, extract something from you, or weigh you...all of which can be traumatic!

But I realized my body was weakening. I had to fight to stay alert. Within the hour, we were in an exam room ready to get to the root of what was attacking my health. A kind, young physician greeted me. He listened to my story and referred me to a local hospital for a series of blood tests.

Now, a few hours later, a woman's voice on the phone told me the test results were in. Her tone implied they were not good.

My Personal Journal of Hope

Romans 4:19 tells us that Abraham, "without weakening in his faith...faced the fact that his body was as good as dead—since he was about a hundred years old." Facing overwhelming facts is not a sign of weak faith. In fact, true faith is "sincere" and "unfeigned" (see 2 Tim. 1:5 NIV and KJV, respectively). It does not pretend or ignore the facts.

What are some of the overwhelming facts you are facing at this moment in your life?

Romans 4:20-21 goes on to tell us Abraham "did not waver through unbelief regarding the promise of God, but was strengthened in his faith and gave glory to God, being fully persuaded that God had power to do what He had promised."

Without ignoring the facts, cite some of the even more overwhelming promises God has made to you:

_____

_____

_____

_____

_____

_____

CHAPTER 2

Held by Hope

In your distress you called
and I rescued you
(Psalm 81:7a).

The 15-minute trip across town to this unknown doctor's office seemed to take forever. Alone in the car, incessant questions whirled inside my head. Fear of the unknown began to play scenarios in the theater of my mind. A sense of dread was crawling through the windows of my imagination. *What is happening to me? Why was it so urgent for me to see a doctor tonight? Why didn't the woman on the phone tell me more?*

My thoughts raced to my wife Sheri. In our pre-cell phone existence, I was unable to get in touch with her. How I wanted her to be with me now! What would she think when she returned home to decipher the sparse information I had given our daughter?

Sheri is the joy of my life. We crossed paths at Messiah College in 1974. Across a crowded cafeteria, our eyes met.

At least I imagined they met. I was looking at her. But I think she was looking at the menu posted above my head.

A few days later, we ended up at the same table during a random-drawing freshmen orientation dinner. We connected immediately, talking to each other continually throughout the meal. I enjoyed every moment. For years I found myself nervous when talking to girls. Face-to-face encounters with them were laborious. Telephone calls were terrifying. Lulls in conversation seemed like eternities so I would keep a running list of topics to discuss on a tablet beside the phone. But Sheri was different. She was easy to talk to and fun to listen to. I didn't want the night to end.

Having several of the same classes, we continually crossed paths. I was fascinated with this brown-eyed, enthusiastic lover of life. She was deeply devoted to Jesus, talking about Him and to Him like He was right there in the room. And every time I was with her, I sensed His presence.

Although I was a follower of Jesus, I realized that much of my relationship with Him consisted of external rules without internal joy. She taught me how to talk with Him and how to hear His voice.

Sheri made me long for more of Jesus.

In a short time, I found myself plunging into deeper rivers of His vibrant presence. Learning to live a lifestyle of constant immersion in the Holy Spirit, I more and more came to experience the life that Jesus died for me to have. And I loved every minute of it.

With Sheri and others, I spent increasing time in the Lord's presence. We worshiped Him—not just singing songs about Him, but singing *to* Him. We could sense His pleasure.

I also learned to pray. Sheri taught me to ask the Lord for more than a blessing on a meal and traveling mercies on the highway. She prayed Bible-sized prayers. History-changing, world-shaking prayers. We asked for things like "a spirit of revelation" so we could know Him better. We cried out for revival. For miracles. For a whole generation of passionate followers of Jesus to arise on the earth. This woman rocked my world. And I found that I really liked being with her.

For much of that first year at college, we were just friends who hung around with other mutual friends. Then one day my roommate gave me one of those "Yeah, right!" looks. Larry "The Weasel" Wetzel had a way of seeing through things. And he could see through me. A no-nonsense Bible major from Gettysburg, he was just the kind of roommate I needed. I could never hide a thing from him. He could tell what I was thinking—and especially where I had stashed my mother's chocolate chip cookies!

I admitted to myself that I was crazily committed to loving this woman for the rest of my life. When I confessed my love to Sheri, I expected fireworks in the sky. Two people running through a field of daisies, falling into each other's arms. Instead, my daydreams were interrupted with, "Oh, I'll have to pray about that."

I liked that about her.

I still do.

I married Sheri in the summer of 1978. Next to giving my heart to Jesus, it is the best thing I have ever done.

Wishing she was with me now, I pulled into the doctor's parking lot at 8:00 that Monday evening. The fall sky had already grown dim, and the wind rustled dry leaves on the trees, giving the night an eerie feeling.

I opened the door and walked into the deserted waiting room. Most of the office staff had gone home for the day.

I mustered a squeaky "Hello," my voice breaking like a junior high school boy. I heard the sound of determined steps marching my way, echoing on the tile floor.

Doctor Kathy greeted me with a warm handshake and a concerned look. As she led me to one of the examination rooms, we passed a few remaining staff members who briefly looked up from piles of paperwork. Only then did I see the sign on the wall. *Oncologist.*

A cancer doctor!

Do I have cancer?

The next moment I was seated on an exam table covered with white crinkly paper, wondering what I was about to hear.

Doctor Kathy made some initial statements about my blood test results. She spoke of procedures they had completed, etc., etc., etc. I didn't understand much of her explanation. I began to wish I had paid closer attention in my high school biology class or watched a few more episodes of "Marcus Welby, M.D."

Then she said it: "Mr. Hess, you have cancer."

There. The mystery was out in the open.

I have heard of the stages people go through when facing something traumatic. Shock. Denial. Anger. I think I went through all of them simultaneously.

Doctor Kathy went on, "You have leukemia, a cancerous attack on the parts of your body that manufacture blood." In the following minutes, I learned that most, if not all, of my white cells were immature blast cells, weak and unable to fight infections. I had an overabundance of these deficient cells and only a minimal amount of platelets, the blood cells that cause clotting. This explained the excessive bruising and bleeding I was experiencing. My red blood cells were also replaced and outnumbered by unhealthy white cells. Since red blood cells carry oxygen throughout the body, without them my oxygen levels had depleted. As a result, I was constantly tired.

She continued, "We were hoping to find that we were dealing with chronic leukemia, a slowly progressing disease that has been very treatable. But you have acute myeloid leukemia, a type that progresses rapidly. We will do all we can. We'd like to admit you to the hospital tonight to begin chemotherapy treatment immediately."

I asked her to give me one more night at home.

"I have to tell my family. I have to pray."

She graciously conceded. "But you must be here at 7:00 tomorrow morning for a bone marrow test." (That sounded like a great way to start the day!)

Doctor Kathy and one of her colleagues showed me to the door. They both hugged me warmly. And I stepped out into the night.

I stood alone in the empty parking lot for a few moments. The brisk November wind mirrored the storm that was brewing in my soul. *What would I tell my family?*

I could see their faces. Bethany, the oldest, was a confident leader in her own right. She would tackle this as a challenge to overcome. Already, as I would learn in a few moments, she had come to certain conclusions about my health and had rallied a spontaneous prayer gathering that was forming at our house.

Ben, the middle child, was 12 at the time. He was the thoughtful, compassionate one. Though he used fewer words than the others in the family, his wheels of observation and insight were constantly in motion.

Brandon, the 9-year-old, energetic last-born, had the spontaneous exuberance of his mother. Constantly in motion, he was either making music or making his brother and sister laugh. He was born "outside the box," and there he would thrive.

Sheri, my wife of 19 years, would feel this the most. Externally, she would rise to the occasion. She had filled our children with hope and encouragement, serving as everyone's cheerleader. And she would do so once again. Deep inside, though, I saw the frightened daughter who knew how to find strength in her Father's arms.

"I'm shocked!" I heard myself say out loud into the night air.

I'm not! A still, small voice whispered inside my spirit. *Besides,* I heard the voice of Jesus say, *I have prepared you for this moment!*

Then, like a lightning bolt coursing through a storm, the voice of the Holy Spirit filled me with reminders of His presence. Scripture verses came as steady waves upon my soul:

> *Why are you cast down, O my soul? And why are you disquieted within me? Hope in God, for I shall yet praise Him* (Psalm 42:5 NKJV).

> *I will never leave you nor forsake you* (Hebrews 13:5b NKJV).

> *I am the Lord, the God of all mankind. Is anything too hard for Me?* (Jeremiah 32:27)

> *With man, this is impossible. But with God, all things are possible* (Matthew 19:26).

I cried. Not a cry of despair, but a cry of gratitude. I was overwhelmed by the sense of His nearness to me in this storm.

I walked to the car, prepared to face my family. Paul's words about being "perplexed, but not in despair" (2 Cor. 4:8) began to take on a whole new meaning.

I was perplexed.

But my heart was being held by Hope.

My Personal Journal of Hope

Paul spoke openly about the difficult situations he faced in his life. He said he was "perplexed, but not in despair" (2 Cor. 4:8).

Perplexed means "to be in doubt, to not know which way to turn, to not know how to decide or what to do."[1]

What perplexing concerns are pressing upon you at this time?

_____

_____

_____

_____

_____

_____

Not in despair means that, despite perplexing feelings, we are "not utterly at a loss, not destitute of resources, or renouncing all hope."[2]

What resources are you trusting the Lord to supply you with in these puzzling moments?

_____

_____

_____

_____

_____

_____

_____

ENDNOTES

1. Thayer's Greek Definitions.
2. Ibid.

CHAPTER 3

The Open Door

*I will return her vineyards to her
and transform the Valley of Trouble
into a gateway of hope*
(Hosea 2:15a NLT).

Certain geographic locations have memories—good or bad—associated with them: fruit of events that happened there. Think about Gettysburg. Jerusalem. Hiroshima. Columbine. Jericho. The World Trade Center. The Upper Room.

Such was the case for a place known as the Valley of Achor. *Achor!* Just to hear it mentioned sent chills down the spine of all who remembered. *Achor* is a Hebrew word meaning "troubling" or "to be disturbed," given after the execution by stoning of a man named Achan and his family. Achan was one of Joshua's key military leaders who brought trouble upon Israel because of his open defiance of the Lord. By keeping spoils from Israel's defeat of Jericho, Achan violated God's clear warning. Because he hid treasures from Jericho in his tent, Achan caused the loss of

Israelite lives. He also opened the door for a humiliating military defeat at the city of Ai. "That place has been called the Valley of Achor ever since" (Josh. 7:26), forever remembered as the "place of trouble." A valley of death and defeat. A place of hopelessness.

Yet the prophet Hosea saw a picture of the Lord stepping into the Valley of Achor, the very place of troubling and tears. He heard the promise of the Lord, spoken from His heart to those in a time of overwhelming difficulty:

> *I will allure her, bring her into the wilderness and speak kindly to her. Then I will give her her vineyards from there, and the valley of Achor as a door of hope. And she will sing there as in the days of her youth* (Hosea 2:14-15 NASB).

And in this valley of tears, that same Lord was opening a door of hope for me.

As I turned the corner of our street and drove toward the house, I noticed a number of cars in our driveway. Opening the door from the garage, I was welcomed by a kitchen filled with family and friends. Waves of love broke over me as I walked through the door. My parents-in-law were there, along with my sister-in-law Robin. Our friend Karna and our youth pastor Tom had also rallied to the call. Upon hearing a vague report that something might be wrong, they had dropped everything to stand with us in prayer. A cavalcade of phone calls was already alerting others to pray. Within a few short hours, a small army was sounding the battle cry.

Questioning looks encircled the room. I wanted to give all of them answers. But glimpsing at the faces of Sheri and the children, I drew them aside to tell them first.

Crouching to look at them eye-to-eye, I heard myself say, "Daddy has cancer. But Jesus has Daddy."

Together we melted into one big hug, mixed with tears. We felt hands on our heads and shoulders as those we love lifted us up to the One who loves. We embraced one another, and we sensed His embrace.

After tucking the children into bed, I attempted to explain in my own non-scientific way what the doctor had told me. *Leukemia. A blood disease. A hospital stay. How long? Chemotherapy?*

We had decisions to make and a short time in which to make them. Again, we prayed. Sheri and I sensed the Lord telling us that He would lead us with His peace. He assured us we would know in a deeply settled way what He was calling us to do.

As friends and family milled around the kitchen, I slipped off to the computer room. Whether it was the nervous energy or a father's sense of duty, I don't know. I found myself typing some final pages on Ben's sixth grade science project—"The Effects of Acid Rain on Plant Life." I wasn't sure what lay ahead of me on this journey, but I wanted to tie up some loose ends before I took the next step. Besides, it gave me something else to think about.

A few days later, reflecting on this moment, I would write these words in my journal:

> What a whirlwind this has been. Yet, what a wonderful "eye" in this storm. Promises abound in this time. Scriptures and personal words keep coming to me with the constant and sweet reminding of the Holy Spirit. There *is* a door of Hope in this valley of troubling! I am watching as the Lord wars against my demonic enemies (Nahum 1:2-6). At the same time, He is fortifying me with His peace, His faith, and His presence (Nahum 1:7-10). Keep rejoicing!

Habakkuk 3:19 in the Amplified Bible says:

The Lord God is my strength, my personal bravery, and my invincible army...and will make me to walk [not to stand still in terror, but to walk] and make [spiritual] progress upon my high places [of trouble, suffering, or responsibility].

That night I slept like a child, safe in the arms of my Father. He is my strength. *He is my personal bravery. He is my invincible army. I will not stand still in terror. Instead, I will make spiritual progress upon my high places of trouble.* These words ran through my mind and out of my mouth. I meditated on them—in the true meaning of the word *meditate*, which means to "mutter or talk to yourself." (The false notions of Eastern mysticism say meditation is allowing your mind to be blank, in a neutral state. Instead, Scripture describes meditation as having your mind filled with truth, in an active state.) The more I meditated on the Father's promises to me, the more He filled my heart with His peace.

At one point I awoke with the sense that someone was watching me. Through hazy eyes I saw Sheri's face on the pillow smiling at me.

"We're going to make it. We're going through," she whispered confidently.

She then reminded me of an encounter we had several months before. "Remember the word we received at the Morningstar conference?" she asked, a quiet boldness in every word.

Immediately it came to me!

We had attended a conference in Charlotte earlier that year, hosted by Rick Joyner and Morningstar ministries.

One afternoon we signed up for a time of prophetic prayer with a team Rick's ministry had trained.

As we entered our designated meeting room, we greeted the team members. Though they were strangers to us, within moments we found ourselves connected to their hearts as we together sought after His heart. A variety of timely words of insight and encouragement were shared that day. As we were about to leave, one of the men spoke, "The devil is about to make a grave tactical error with you, sir." Pointing to me, he continued, "I see a door opening to a very dark corridor. After you walk through this corridor, you will come out the other side stronger than ever. What you receive from the Lord in the middle of this darkness will not only strengthen you, but you will strengthen others as well. This attack will have a boomerang effect on the kingdom of darkness."

At the time we heard these words, we had no idea what the meaning could be. We took some random guesses, yet none seemed to fit. But that night it began to make sense. It became a word in season. That night the season began.

The Lord gives us this insight into the nature of His words to us:

> As the rain and the snow come down from heaven...so is My word that goes out from My mouth: it will not return to Me empty, but will accomplish what I desire and achieve the purpose for which I sent it (Isaiah 55:10-11).

The word of the Lord sometimes falls upon us like the rain. Immediately we receive it. In the moment it is given, we understand as He speaks to our current situation, and it becomes water to our souls.

At other times His words fall like snow. They may hit us "cold" in the moment. They may rest high in the mountains, seeming distant or lofty. They may even confuse us at the time we hear them. Yet His promises wait for the appointed time. Like snow in the hills melting in the springtime and flooding the valley below, so His word from the past can one day come alive in our present.

So it was with this word.

The snow was melting, making His promises life to us.

Though we suddenly found ourselves forced into a dark corridor, we could clearly see that the Lord had gone ahead of us, opening a door of hope.

My Personal Journal of Hope

Habakkuk 3:19 in the Amplified Bible says:

The Lord God is my strength, my personal bravery, and my invincible army...and He will make me walk [not stand still in terror, but walk] and make [spiritual] progress upon my high places [of trouble, suffering, and responsibility].

As you meditate on these promises, how does your heart respond to them?

What do you hear the Lord saying to you through these words?

HOPE BEYOND REASON

Ask the Holy Spirit to remind you of past words, dreams, pictures, or any other impressions He gave to you in days gone by. Though they may not have made sense to you then, they may have powerful applications now.

How has He prepared you for the moment you are now facing?

_____

_____

_____

_____

_____

_____

HOPE BEYOND REASON

CHAPTER 4

Eyes of Love

> *When you pass through the waters, I will be with*
> *you; and when you pass through the rivers, they*
> *will not sweep over you. When you walk through*
> *the fire, you will not be burned...For I am the Lord*
> *your God.... Do not be afraid, for I am with you*
> (Isaiah 43:2-3a, 5a).

Tuesday morning came like a shot. Shaved, showered, and packed, I found myself at 7:00 A.M. lying on a crinkly-papered examination table receiving a bone marrow test. What I thought would be an X-ray turned out to be needles. Several of them. I would learn over the next several months that needles would become a normal part of my life. As I lay on my side facing the wall, the doctor extracted bone marrow from my hipbone in my lower back. And I prayed. A lot.

A few moments later, I was admitted to the hospital. The name of the hospital? *Holy Spirit Hospital.* (I kid you not.) It was yet another nod from the Father that He was in charge.

Because of my compromised immune system, I was admitted to a private room that would become my home for the next six months. I came to know each ceiling tile in this room by name and was sure I could re-paint the pictures on the walls while blindfolded. It was a pleasant room. And it was all mine. But it wasn't home.

Since Holy Spirit Hospital is a Catholic facility, a crucifix hung on the wall just inside my door. To be honest, it startled me a bit. Being raised Protestant, I had never been that close to a crucifix before. The image of Jesus hanging on the cross stirred ancient memories for me. I recalled the words of one of my junior high Sunday school teachers. "The Catholics have it all wrong," she would state. "They keep Jesus on the cross, when He's actually risen from the dead!" It was one of those statements that sounded good at the time but proved shallow the more you thought about it. Since this crucifix hung across from my bathroom door, I had multiple encounters with it on a daily basis. Instead of a foreign icon, it became an inspiring reminder—I was loved. With the greatest love the world has ever known. It was as if Jesus was saying to me, "I carried it all. All of your sin. All of your sorrow. And all of your sickness. By My suffering, you are healed."

From my window, I had an open view of the city of Harrisburg, the capital of our state. This room was to become my prayer station for this season of my life. And asking God to heal and restore our city became my daily cry.

The cancer ward nursing staff was excellent. Both compassionate and proficient, most of these nurses had committed many years of their lives to serving on this unit. My stay exposed me to an unsung army who quietly serves and gives of themselves daily. Their battlefield is marked by the smell of cleaning supplies...the sounds of medical carts clanging and scooting and bumping the walls...the voice of the "loudspeaker lady" at a microphone somewhere paging doctors and announcing endless meetings...and the moans of patients wrestling with their pain, crying out for someone to ease their agony. These pieces of my new environment would take some getting used to. And yet, this was normal life for this hospital team. My admiration for them grew daily.

That evening I underwent surgery to install a Hickman catheter in my chest, a port through which chemotherapy would be administered. When I awoke, I was stunned to find what looked like speaker cords hanging out of my chest. I looked like the Terminator on a bad day.

By Wednesday evening, chemotherapy treatment had begun. This first round of chemo would continue non-stop for 7 days, 24 hours of each day. Bags of various colored drugs were hung on a portable pole. They were then fed through a machine attached to the pole into the tubes in my chest. The front of the machine looked like a face, re-minding me of the robot maid on *The Jetsons* cartoon show I had watched as a kid. I affectionately named this pole contraption "Matilda." Since we were permanently at-tached, we waltzed together regularly from bathroom to hallway to bedside.

And so a new routine had begun for me. With Matilda in tow, I would complete my morning hygiene regimen, then travel to the laundry cart to pick out a fresh designer hos-pital gown for the day. I'm not sure who is responsible for designing these "gowns." They felt more like over-sized bibs—wide open in the back. My guess is that their real function is to aid in patient security. Dressed like that, who would want to leave their bed?

Over the next several days, I met the nursing staff one by one, shift by shift. Each was special, but I felt especially drawn to one of them. Her name was Rosemary. She had been nursing most of her life. During one of our daily con-versations, she told me she was considering retirement soon.

Rosemary was somewhat of a challenge for me to unravel. She seemed to have a tough exterior but a tender, guarded heart. At times I thought she would have liked to avoid me if she could. Phasing in and out of groggy hours, I found myself moved to pray for her. I asked Jesus to give me insight into her life.

One day I asked, "So what do you think of preachers?"

One look told me what she was thinking.

"I don't like them," she snapped. "They're usually mean. And rude. And most of all, condescending," she said curtly. "They've been some of the worst patients I have ever had. They yell at you; then they want to preach at you!"

I told her how saddened I was to hear this. Then I apologized on behalf of the many pastors I knew who would not treat someone this way.

On another occasion, Rosemary opened the door to her past a little more. I asked her when she became interested in health care. Through watery eyes, she spoke of her physician father. "He died of leukemia," she said matter-of-factly. "He diagnosed himself," she paused, "and died a horrible death."

I didn't answer her right away. She wasn't looking for answers. She wanted someone to hear her heart—for someone claiming to represent Jesus to do something other than preach at her. She was looking for someone to care. And listen.

Here I was, a preacher with leukemia, right under her nose. I was a daily reminder of one of the most painful experiences of her life. I had nowhere else to go and nothing else to do, so I asked Jesus to help me help her. I really needed His help.

I told Rosemary that I had been preaching for almost 20 years, but at the moment I was "preached out." If she wanted someone to listen, I told her I would be here.

Over the weeks to come, I watched her heart soften.

One day she came to me and said, "If the offer still stands, I'll take you up on it." From that day on, she frequently took one of her breaks in my room. She drank coffee. I drank water through a "bendy straw." And I listened.

In those moments, my grandmother's words came back to me. She would often say, "The good Lord gave us two ears and one mouth so we would spend twice as much time listening as we do talking." Ah, the sage wisdom of grandmothers! James must have had a wise grandmother, too. He wrote: "Everyone should be quick to listen, slow to speak and slow to become angry" (James 1:19). Solomon's words also instructed my heart afresh as I sat with Rosemary day to day: "A fool does not delight in understanding, but only in revealing his own mind" (Prov. 18:2 NASB). I remembered these words and knew I was being called to live them.

As healing as timely words can be, attentive listening also has the power to restore people. There is a time to speak, but there is also a time to keep silent. I was learning to listen. And I was learning to care about people in a whole new way.

Without love, people become objects to us. They either become machinery we maneuver to get what we want, or they become scenery we merely observe, never caring to look beneath the surface. During my coffee breaks with Rosemary, my chats with Sylvia the morning shift cleaning lady, and my discussions with doctors about *their* lives, *their* families, and *their* conditions—in all of these encounters, Jesus was teaching me to love. He was healing my soul.

In the day-to-day running of our lives, we seldom stop to assess how we are *really* living. The automatic response to the trite greeting "How are you doing?" is usually the equally trite "Good!" or "Can't complain!" Now with the brakes slammed in my life, I had a golden opportunity—a gift from the Lord—to take a good look at how I was really doing. And I didn't like everything I saw.

I would never have considered myself unloving. After all, I was a pastor. And pastors become pastors because they care about people. *Right?*

There I lay with time on my hands and people in and out of my room constantly. I didn't have the luxury of retreating to my study and burying myself in books, or shielding myself behind my Bible. I had to face people. And I had to face myself. Both scenarios were scary.

Healing does not begin in our bodies; it starts in our souls. Jesus breaks the power of our sin and our selfishness just as powerfully as He breaks the power of our diseases. He wants us to "prosper and be in good health, just as [our] soul prospers" (3 John 2 NASB). He wanted to heal my body. But He wanted to restore my soul, too.

I hadn't become unloving overnight. It happened gradually. Like rings growing around the trunk of a tree, I had insulated myself from others, layer by layer. Offenses attached themselves over the years. Offensive things happen to all of us. I had chosen not to forgive some of them. People had hurt me. And no one was going to hurt me like that again. I thought I was punishing them. Instead, I was torturing myself.

I have heard it said that unforgiveness is like drinking poison and expecting your enemy to die. Jesus said that when we do not forgive our offenders, *we* become the ones tortured by our own bitterness (see Matt. 18:34-35 KJV).

There at the hospital in a flurry of medical treatments and procedures, a supernatural operation was taking place in my heart. I was learning to forgive. I was learning to see people as Jesus sees them. I was beginning to look at others through His eyes of love.

And the torment stopped.

My Personal Journal of Hope

Take a look at the people the Lord has surrounded you with at this point in your journey.

Think about the ones He has given to strengthen and encourage you. As you gratefully ponder each one of them, reflect on their contributions to your life.

What messages has the Lord sent to you through them?

_____

_____

_____

_____

_____

_____

How has He touched your life through their lives?

HOPE BEYOND REASON

Part of Job's healing came as he prayed for his friends (see Job 42:10). These "friends" had said many ridiculous, even offensive, things to him. Yet as Job chose to overlook their hurtful words and pray for their hearts, healing came to his own heart.

Ask the Lord to show you the people He wants you to minister to. Ask Him for insights into their lives that will help you to touch their hearts.

How does He lead you to pray for them?

_____

_____

_____

_____

_____

_____

What impressions come to your mind as you are around them?

CHAPTER 5

Prayer Warriors

I will not die but live, and will
proclaim what the Lord has done
(Psalm 118:17).

My hair began to fall out. It didn't happen all at once, but as the days passed, it began to look like a small, shedding dog was sharing my pillow each night. I called a barber friend of mine. David came in one evening and finished the job chemo had begun. Unlike his usual meticulous haircut, within moments David's clippers made short order of what was left of my hair. I gained a new appreciation for the nakedness sheep feel the day after they have donated to the blanket fund. Shivering as I fell asleep, I wondered how long it would be until I would need a barber again.

With my freshly shaved "Elmer Fudd" look, I frightened myself in the mirror the next morning. I missed my hair. I felt every breeze that moved through the room at night, making it hard to sleep. Sheri put out a call for hats. Boy, did we get hats! They came in all shapes and sizes. I had a hat for almost every day of the month. My favorite was a white baseball cap, a gift from Pastor John Shuey. On the front it said, "Bad Hair Day."

The hair on my face had also stopped growing, eliminating the need for shaving. In fact, my morning hygiene routine was suddenly reduced to blinking, splashing, and brushing my teeth. My eyebrows and eyelashes eventually took their leave of absence, too. *Suddenly, I was half the man I used to be*[1]

Sheri was a constant support. Every day she would see the children off to school and then make her way into the hospital. My heart would leap as I recognized the rhythm of her footsteps in the hallway. I would often hear her humming a song as she came toward the room, bringing the day's mail with her. Letters and cards of encouragement meant so much to us.

One day a 13-year-old girl named Mary stepped into our lives. She had urged her mother to bring her to the hospital to see us, saying she had something she needed to tell us. Mary had been diagnosed with ovarian cancer earlier that year. A large tumor had been removed, yet doctors were uncertain about her chances for a full recovery. One day while reading her Bible, Mary came across this verse in Psalms:

> *I will not die but live, and will proclaim what the Lord has done* (Psalm 118:17).

It spoke hope to her in her valley of trouble. Here she stood beside my bed, cancer-free. The tumor was gone, and Mary's life had been restored. She lived, and she was telling me what the Lord had done. Mary held out a hand-written note card with Psalm 118:17 printed on it. "I hung this by my bed when I was in the hospital," she said with a sparkle in her eyes. "It gave me hope. I want you to have hope, too. You're not going to die. You're going to live, too!"

Then she prayed for us. Her words were pure expressions of trust, voiced to a God she had found to be trustworthy.

With a confident smile, Mary looked at me and said once more, "You will not die. You will live. And you will tell everyone what the Lord has done."

After Mary and her mother left the room, Sheri opened the mail. Included in all the expressions of support were *five* cards with Psalm 118:17 written in them. The Lord's faithful promises were calling us to a deeper place of trust! "I will not die but live, and will proclaim what the Lord has done."

Together we laughed. It was not the laughter of a humorous diversion. Rather it was a confident laughter, given to us as a gift from the Lord, born out of the relief that comes from knowing we can trust Him. He was showering us with reminders of His strong presence to sustain us. The Bible frequently says that the Lord brings confirmation through two or three witnesses. We had received a word confirmed by six witnesses! I guess we needed all of them.

Later that day, I wrote these words in my journal:

> The Lord's strength has been wonderful! For years I have thought the laughter that brings strength to the bone and marrow (in Proverbs 17:22) has been humor. But it is not. Rather, it is the victorious laughter of God in the face of the idle threats of the enemy.

Much of humor finds amusement in the absurd. Yet heavenly laughter reverberates with the certainty of Jesus' victory!

On her way home that evening, Sheri noticed that the lights were on at the church and the parking lot was filled with cars. She knew of no scheduled meeting, so she pulled in, curious to see what was going on. As she entered the sanctuary, she was amazed to see hundreds of people engaged in prayer.

At the front of the church was our dear friend Dawn Sweigart leading the charge. Dawn had surrendered her life to Jesus just a few years prior. She had come to Him with a wide-open heart that seemed to blossom overnight. She was a leader, an influencer, a motivator, and a budding prophet. She heard the voice of the Lord and sensed His heartbeat in an extremely unique way. She expressed it in an equally distinctive way. We deeply loved her.

Just moments after learning the news of my illness, she rallied hundreds of people from our church and our region to pray. As a young follower of Jesus, Dawn had taken hold of His promises with tenacity. If He said He would do miracles, then *He would do miracles!* If He said we would do greater works than He did (see John 14:12), then *we will do greater works than He did!* Her heart throbbed with the conviction that *He will make His promises a reality in our day!*

Dawn had organized round-the-clock prayer for us. People volunteered to pray for an hour each week, collectively covering all 168 hours of the week. Local pastors and their congregations joined us, and various prayer gatherings spontaneously sprang up in response to the needs of the moment and the Holy Spirit's leading. This is what Jesus said His Church would look like. More than buildings, organizations, politics, or programs, He builds His Church with people. He draws those who are being rescued and restored, as well as those now devoting their lives to rescuing and restoring others.

There is nothing more beautiful on the planet than when followers of Jesus act like Jesus. On the other hand, there is nothing more grievous than when believers in Jesus don't even resemble Him. Some like to throw stones at the Church in moments like these, seeing her as detestable. Out of touch. Past her prime. But as author Fawn Parish quips, "The Church is like Noah's ark. It stinks but it's the only thing afloat." She goes on to say, "When we criticize the Church, we are criticizing something Jesus adores and spilled His blood for. It is His own precious possession."[2]

Night after night these prayer warriors met. Often sharing in communion, they would declare the power of Jesus' victory over sin, sickness, death, and all of the forces of hell. They spent hours together worshiping, encouraging one another, and interceding.

But they were not just praying for me. They were asking the Lord to touch every life in our region and beyond!

Steve Boyer, one of our pastors, stopped by my room to videotape a message from me to the church. Surprised to see my bald head, he told me some people would be disappointed. Reading First Samuel 14:45, they had learned of people asking that Jonathan, King Saul's son, would not die. In addition, they had begged that "not a hair of his head will fall to the ground." As a result, our church family was praying that not one hair of *my* head would be removed.

Touched by their tenacity, I wanted to encourage them on the tape. As the camera began to roll, I felt inspired to lean forward and give the lens an aerial view of my empty scalp. As Steve zoomed in, I said, "Don't be discouraged by the fact that I have temporarily lost my hair. What the enemy intends for evil, the Lord will use for His good. Let's do this: Let's claim that 100 people will come to know Jesus Christ for every hair that has fallen from my head." I then pointed to various sections of my head, naming counties and towns in our region. "As the water covers the sea," I continued, "people in all of these places will know Him in His fullness!" As I spoke, I meant every word. And I still do.

Although I had spoken this in the spur of the moment, we received this charge as a faith challenge from the Lord. To this day, many refer to it as a pivotal moment in their prayer lives. Faith and fervency erupted in people's hearts throughout the congregation. Many who did not see themselves as prayer warriors boldly enlisted in this holy war. It was an all-out fight for the hearts and lives of those in our territory. Mindful of the eternal consequences, we continue to pray for every orphaned heart to know and receive the love of their Father through His amazing Son Jesus!

What could have intimidated us, ignited us.

Fresh doors of hope were being opened in this valley of trouble.

ENDNOTES

1. The Beatles, "Yesterday."

2. Fawn Parish, *Honor: What Love Looks Like* (Ventura, CA: Renew Books, 1999), 86.

My Personal Journal of Hope

The gift of hope enables us to see beyond the difficult moments, giving us a bigger picture of what the Lord is doing in and through us.

Isaiah 53 gives a detailed description of Jesus' moments of suffering on the cross. In His hours of intense warfare, He received the revelation that "after the suffering of His soul, He will see the light of life and be satisfied...[He] will justify many, and He will bear their iniquities" (Isa. 53:11). Hebrews 12 gives us additional insight into His heart, stating that "for the joy set before Him [He] endured the cross" (Heb. 12:2).

Ask the Lord to give you a fresh revelation of His bigger picture for your life.

What unfulfilled promises and dreams does He remind you of?

HOPE BEYOND REASON

Just because we face momentary trials does not mean that the purposes of God for us need to be put on hold.

Which dimensions of His call on your life can you walk in right now?

_____

_____

_____

_____

_____

_____

HOPE BEYOND REASON

Chapter 6

Invasion of Courage

For He will command His angels concerning you to guard you in all your ways; they will lift you up in their hands, so that you will not strike your foot against a stone (Psalm 91:11-12).

The Lord will grant that the enemies who rise up against you will be defeated before you. They will come at you from one direction but flee from you in seven (Deuteronomy 28:7).

We are always in the middle of a spiritual battle, though its intensity varies from minor skirmish to full-fledged war. Sometimes the reality of this warfare becomes more evident to us than at other times. Though struggles with other human beings may rank among our greatest agitations, there is more going on than meets our natural eyes. As Paul stated clearly, "We are not fighting against flesh-and-blood enemies, but against evil rulers and authorities of the unseen world" (Eph. 6:12a NLT).

This battle with cancer was one of those times.

I cannot remember a season when I felt as physically and emotionally weary as I did then. I had been told that chemotherapy makes you feel like you've been body-slammed by a battalion of NFL linebackers. Actually, I felt like I had been run over by a herd of bison which then backed up and tried it a few more times.

My body was weak from the loss of red cells. It took all of my energy to get from the bed to the bathroom, a trip made frequently throughout the day and night. With all of the liquids being constantly poured into me, I had become a human "Mr. Coffee" machine.

My sense of taste was gone, replaced by a constant metal-lic flavor. Because everything I ate had the distinct taste of aluminum, most days I ate very little. I was losing weight rapidly. The concerned staff kept encouraging me to eat. The only food I could tolerate was Rice Krispies and some con-traband Chinese dinners smuggled in by my parents.

The most grueling physical effect was not the seven days of intensive chemotherapy. Instead, it was the trans-fusion treatment that followed.

Chemotherapy has been described as pushing the "reset" button on your body's blood manufacturing plant. With its goal of removing unhealthy blast cells (immature white cells) from your system, it also depletes the body's red blood cells and platelets (blood clotting agents). The result is a severe loss of energy, coupled with an inability to clot. Being confined to my room and having no facial hair kept me from my two greatest enemies: overexertion and sharp objects. Although I felt miserable, I was safe.

At the conclusion of my first round of chemo, I required a blood transfusion to replenish my red cell count. This type of transfusion usually involves receiving the blood from a single donor. If your body accepts the blood, then you are in the clear. If it doesn't like the blood, it lets you know right away. Cold sweats. Hot flashes. High fevers. A basic body temper tantrum follows.

I received my first blood transfusion with minimal reactions. However, I also needed a platelet transfusion. Platelets are different creatures altogether. While blood transfusions come from one donor, platelets are harvested from multiple donors. If your body does not like the DNA of just one of the donors, it works to reject the entire package.

With my first platelet transfusion, my body went ballistic. I spiked a high fever and shook uncontrollably. One moment I was freezing, and the next I was burning up. During the night, it got even worse.

The nurses introduced me to a device known as "the cooling blanket." Its purpose was to lower my fever from the 103-degree range back to normal. The concept sounded soothing. *Cooling* — a refreshing experience. *Blanket* — a comforting experience. Put them together and what do you have? A modern-day torture apparatus!

Lying on this ice-cold, full-body-length, water-filled rubber mat while sporting my designer hospital gown was an experience I never want to revisit. You could have simultaneously fried an egg on my head while chilling ice cubes on my back. I felt like one giant baked Alaska!

Yet beyond the physical weariness, a war was raging against my mind and emotions. Unrelenting thoughts assaulted my brain. Though I had heard that high fevers and hallucinations often go hand-in-hand, I knew that there was more going on here than mere physical reactions. This was a *fight*. I kept reminding myself that our spiritual battles are called a *good* fight, not a *bad* fight (see 1 Tim. 6:12; 2 Tim. 4:7). Though the struggles can be intense, Jesus will always lead us into victory (see 2 Cor. 2:14).

One arena I battled in was *time*. Suddenly I had a lot of it on my hands. Pastoring a church had been a full-time activity. Then, in an instant, that part of my life was on hold. We had appointed our youth pastor Tom to take the wheel of the ship. The elders and staff also rose to the occasion. So, I had more time to pray. Time to read. Time to heal. And time to think.

Sometimes I thought too much.

I watched the nurses' eyes as they checked on me. I tried to read what the doctors were saying (and weren't saying). I listened to their tone of voice. I observed their body language as they looked at my chart and then back at me.

"How am I doing?" I would ask.

"About as we expected," would be the reply, although they didn't always tell me *what* they were expecting. Maybe I didn't really want to know.

One day Sheri pulled one of the nurses aside and kindly asked her for her perspective. Reluctantly she offered her opinion, "Dave has responded pretty well to the treatment, but he is a very sick man. He was very sick when he came to us. He has acute leukemia, which is very aggressive. Although he has had his first chemo treatment, we may have caught it too late." Working to maintain her composure, she continued, "I'm not sure he will be around for Christmas." Sheri felt as if the bottom had dropped out of her world.

Tearfully she came into my room and told me the report. And then she prayed. I have heard this dear woman pray thousands of times, but I will never forget the prayer that came from her heart:

> Lord, David has never been mine. He's always been Yours. Whatever You desire to do with his life is up to You. But I don't want to give him up this

easily. You have made promises to us. Promises that have yet to be fulfilled. So I am asking You, as Your daughter, to rescue His life from this attack.

I'm sure she prayed a number of other things that day, but these words are seared in my memory.

She kissed my bald head and smiled. "Good night, my little Chemo-sabee," she said in a Tonto-like voice. Then she turned and walked out of the room.

From my window, I watched her walk across the parking lot to her car.

Alone.

I was proud of her. Sheri spent her days encouraging me and her nights serving the children. Without a complaint, she spent every ounce of energy supporting us. Single-handedly she carried the daily responsibilities of the household and then stood beside me in the spiritual battle for my life. Together we stood in the door of hope in this valley of trouble.

That evening I slept restlessly. At 3:00 A.M. I awoke, unable to continue sleeping.

There is a song that had come to mean a lot to me. I discovered it when my niece Kayla suffered a life-threatening injury to her pancreas from a bicycle accident earlier that year. I appreciated the music of Kirk Franklin and found one of his songs, *My Life Is in Your Hands*, especially uplifting.

I gave Kirk's CD to Kayla during her hospital stay. Later she told me that she would often sing Kirk's song anytime she was afraid.

Later that year, Kayla was miraculously healed from all the effects of her injury.

Unable to come to my room to visit, she gave her copy of Kirk's CD to her father. "You must give this to Uncle David," she insisted. "I want my victory song to become his victory song, too."

I believe I wore out that CD within the first few days. It ministered life and hope to me in the middle of a very dark time. I memorized the words, singing them to myself whenever fear came to visit.

And so this night at 3:00 A.M., exhausted in body and soul, I began to be afraid. According to the Bible, fear is not just an emotion—it's a spirit. This evil spirit of fear wanted to take me on a dark, distorted carnival ride. Pictures began to flash through my mind. I saw Sheri sitting alone at home, mustering all her courage as she paid the bills, and attempting to hold the family together. I saw Bethany in her wedding gown, walking down the aisle. Alone. I saw Ben and Brandon playing pick-up football in the backyard. Alone.

"You are gone. And they are alone," this insidious spirit whispered in my ear.

These haunting thoughts clutched at my mind, feverishly trying to shut the door of hope. So I began to sing Kayla's song of victory:

> I know that I can make it.
> I know that I can stand.
> No matter what may come my way,
> my life is in His hands.
> With Jesus I can make it.
> With Jesus I can stand.
> *No matter what may come my way,*
> *my life is in Your hands.*[1]

I sang it softly but firmly. And then I choked on the words...and on the thoughts.

I was alone in the room, with only a small light bulb glowing under my bed. Fighting back tears, I attempted to sing again, with no success.

Then the door to my room opened. Someone was walking toward my bed, singing in a soothing voice. And she was singing *my song*!

As she stood beside my bed, I saw in the dim light what appeared to be a stately African-American woman. I don't remember much about her facial features, but I will never forget her eyes. They were courageous eyes, brimming with a supernatural strength.

As I looked into them, I felt as if I was receiving a courage transfusion.

She placed her hands behind my head and gently lifted it from the pillow.

And then she sang to me:

> With Jesus you can make it.
> With Jesus you can stand.
> *No matter what may come your way,*
> *your life is in His hands.*

She was singing my song. Singing it when I could no longer find the strength to sing.

Then she prayed for me, speaking in a language I had never heard before. Courage flooded my heart. When she had finished, she gently placed my head back on the pillow, turned, and left the room.

As I lay there, my body began reverberating with hope. Something had happened. The skirmish with fear had ended. The assaulting thoughts had ceased. The words of David rose up in me:

My soul finds rest in God alone; my salvation comes from Him (Psalm 62:1).

I was experiencing the "peace that passes all understanding," and it felt good.

Sometime later, Rosemary came into the room. She was startled to see that I was awake. She was even more startled at my countenance, commenting that I was glowing.

I told her about my night visitor, describing her appearance.

Rosemary informed me that her pharmacy cart had been parked beside my door for the past several hours as she worked her way down the hall distributing pills to the patients. She had seen no other people pass by. "Besides," she ended emphatically, "we don't have any African-American nurses on duty tonight."

Slightly puzzled, I thought, *Imagine that! Someone woke up in the middle of the night and came here just to sing me a song.*

I couldn't wait to tell Sheri. She was equally bewildered at my encounter with the unexpected night visitor. Then, as we opened that day's bundle of letters, we found a card from some of our pastor friends. They told us they were praying for us, mentioning that one of their church members had seen a vision as the church was in prayer that Sunday morning. This woman had written a description of the vision on an offering envelope, which they included in their card.

As I read this woman's words, I began to tremble inside. She wrote:

As we were praying for Dave, I saw that the Lord sent an angel to him in the night. The angel walked into his room, stood by his bed, and lifted his head from the pillow, cradling it like a mother would do to her child. The angel then ministered to him, giving him gifts of courage straight from the Father.

Though I know they surround us, I had never seen an angel before. "Thousands upon thousands" of them gather "in joyful assembly," the Bible says (Heb. 12:22). They have been commissioned by the Lord to "guard [us] in all of [our] ways" and to "lift [us] up in their hands" (Ps. 91:11-12). Though we may not always see them, they are constantly present, on assignment as servants sent by our loving King to help us. And He is opening our eyes and awakening our senses to know that we are never forsaken. It would be foolish to worship angels; only Jesus is worthy of our worship. But it is equally foolish to ignore them when we desperately need their help.

That day I was learning to welcome angels and even to expect their help.

I needed it now more than ever.

With heavenly help, I was guarded from fear. And lifted up in hope.

ENDNOTE

1. Kirk Franklin, "My Life Is in Your Hands."

My Personal Journal of Hope

Despite the fact that trials involve physical, emotional, and interpersonal conflicts, our ultimate battle is a spiritual one. Paul said, "We are not fighting against flesh-and-blood enemies, but against evil rulers and authorities of the unseen world" (Eph. 6:12a NLT).

Ask the Lord to give you His perspective on your situation.

What spiritual enemies are you facing?

_____

_____

_____

_____

_____

_____

How is He instructing you to stand against their attacks?

We are never alone in our battles. The Lord never leaves us. He sends His word to heal and encourage us. He gives His angels orders to guard and strengthen us. He sends His people to refresh us and fight for us.

How has the Lord supplied your greatest needs in these trying days?

CHAPTER 7

Sustaining Hands

The Lord will sustain him on
his sickbed and restore him
from his bed of illness
(Psalm 41:3).

When my mother-in-law heard that some of the medical staff did not expect me to live to see Christmas, she went to work. Janet has a resilient spirit and refused to lose hope in the middle of the battle. She comes from a long line of "pioneer women" who learned to stand up against any odds, with the Lord by their side.

Janet is an amazing teacher of the Word, a songwriter, and a deep lover of Jesus. She also has an extraordinary ability to create artwork out of anything.

One day in early December, she came into my room carrying a four-foot-tall Christmas tree, made from scraps and odds-and-ends. To me, cloistered away from the holiday bustle, it looked as grand as the tree in Rockefeller Center. It even rivaled the wreath made out of bedpans that hung by the nurses' station!

Looking me squarely in the eyes, Janet said, "David, you are going to see Christmas. And not just *this* Christmas. You're going to see so many Christmases, they'll be coming out your ears!" She spoke in her "I'm-your-mother-in-law-so-listen-up" voice, which she reserved for occasions like this. Rarely had she used this tone with me. But when she's right, she's right. And she was right!

Within a few weeks, the doctors told me that the initial tests showed my body was responding to treatment and beginning to manufacture *healthy white cells!* They said I was in remission. But they delivered the message with a stern "don't-get-your-hopes-up" tone.

I got my hopes up anyway.

I was discharged from the hospital the week before Christmas. It was the best present I could have received. The doctors told me I would need to return immediately after the holidays for more chemotherapy. They were also going to prepare me to receive a bone marrow transplant. They said that although I had responded well to chemotherapy, most people do not survive acute leukemia without a marrow transplant.

So, I took my four-foot Christmas tree and went home.

It was good to be home.

The white-walled hospital room had become a bit claustrophobic. The daily sounds of carts and clangs and "paging Doctor So-and-So" were replaced by the familiar resonance of home. The clock ticking. The street traffic. The teapot whistling. The music playing. The dog gently growling at the squirrels dancing on our front lawn.

And the voices and laughter of those I hold most dear.

My top priority was catching up with my children. To keep them from falling behind in their schoolwork and neglecting their other commitments, we had limited them to just a few visits to the hospital each week, and they tried to make the best of every trip. Knowing many of the nuns and nurses by name, they would greet them as they ran by. Bursting into my room, they would climb onto the bed, trying not to sit on the tubes that surrounded me.

Now reunited at home, we were alone together for the first time in weeks. The children's stories came like torrents. Ben got a perfect score on our acid rain project. His indoor soccer team was winning. Brandon's saxophone playing was improving, sounding more like music and less like a migrating goose. Bethany was learning to drive, thus improving her mother's prayer life. All of this in the course of a few weeks? I looked across the room at Sheri. She was managing this menagerie. And managing me at the same time. My admiration for her, like the Grinch's heart, grew three sizes that day!

We received so many priceless gifts in those days. One of the dearest came from Wanda, a longtime friend of our family. At the onset of this journey, Wanda moved out of her apartment and into our home. From cooking to cleaning to chauffeuring to homework tutoring, she demonstrated laying down your life for your friends. Her sacrificial gift enabled Sheri to spend time with me each day and made our lives a little less crazy.

Extended family and friends came to the house that Christmas week, forming a steady stream of hugs, tears, and prayers. The days were filled with important conversations. Words of encouragement and gratitude were exchanged. Future dreams and goals were shared. The threat of loss had increased our appreciation of one another. Instead of merely spending time together, we savored it. I had come to a new place of valuing my family and friends as priceless treasures. And I told them so.

Though extremely tired, I snuck into the church on the evening of our annual Christmas celebration for the last few minutes of the program. Strolling from the side door onto the stage, I was greeted by gasps of surprise, followed by an eruption of joy. Suddenly the entire room was standing, smiling, crying, and clapping. I was seeing most of them for the first time since my admission to the hospital, and it was a beautiful sight. They looked like royalty. Dressed in their holiday best, a forest of greens and berry reds stretched before me. Little girls in sparkling dresses stood out like ornaments. And then there was Jack, one of our elders, wearing his infamous battery-powered light-up bow tie. For the second time since leaving the hospital, I thought, *It's good to be home.* From the bottom of my heart, with what words I could muster, I attempted to express how much I loved and appreciated them. When words faltered, my tears took over. How blessed I was to grow up in Jesus with these dear friends.

The children and I gathered nightly in the living room for our traditional "Fam-Jam." Piano, guitars, keyboard, saxophone, drums, and any other makeshift instruments we could find were combined to make a joyful noise to the Lord. How I cherished these moments. Though not much of a camera buff, I took scores of mental pictures during this short week at home. These memories composed a gallery I would visit often in the weeks and months to come.

We were newly freed from the constraint of tubes, the constant bustle of nurses, and the persistent cries of beepers and bells. We relished our uninterrupted conversations. Each one of the children had their own unique questions, concerns, and perspectives.

We spoke about faith. About trusting God in the middle of uncertainty. About healing and miracles. Sheri and I reminded them of the promises the Lord had made to us. We talked about the visit from the angel and the amazing love of the One who sends His angels to minister to us.

I looked at each of them and said, "I will not die. I will live. And I will tell everyone about what the Lord has done." Once again, we fell into a family huddle. And we prayed. In the midst of our pain we prayed, allowing Him to fill our hearts with hope. Confiding in Him, we were brought to a new place of confidence. And we rested there.

Harry, our 15-year-old Cairn terrier, was glad to see me, too. I had found him at the Humane Society when he was about seven. Scars from cigarette burns plainly told that he had been sorely abused. He had been thrown from a car, run over by another, and found along the road. Devoted staff had nursed him back to health.

Harry made quite an impression on first sight. Missing several teeth, he had the smile of a jack-o-lantern. He was completely deaf. Like many aging men, he seemed to be compensating for his bald head by growing woolly patches on the sides. Just as I had determined he looked like a mix between Albert Einstein and Larry Fine of the Three Stooges, Harry wagged his tail, licked my hand, and I fell in love.

When Sheri saw him as I carried him to the car, she commented, "Never send a 'mercy man' to pick out a dog!"

When I brought Harry home, the children looked at him and said, "What's that?"

I said, "It's our new dog."

They said, "That's not a dog. It looks like something else." I felt like Charlie Brown with his homely Christmas tree.

Sheri told me that Harry had faithfully stood sentinel by the window for the last month, waiting for me to return. Once home, he stuck to me like glue. During my daily nap, Harry used my chest for his bed, periodically lifting his head, licking my face, and gazing at me in disbelief. Dog breath never smelled so good!

The week passed by quickly. Reluctantly, I packed my small suitcase. I didn't need much, since a whole wardrobe of hospital gowns awaited.

"We're in the Lord's hands," I told the children, heading toward the car for my return trip to the hospital. "He'll take good care of all of us. And I'll be back real soon," I said, a lump forming in my throat as I turned to go.

My Personal Journal of Hope

Gratitude keeps our hearts glued to the Lord's presence. As we thankfully remember Him and all He has done for us, we "enter His gates" (Ps. 100:4), coming into an increased awareness of Him.

Grateful people remember the Lord's faithfulness. They constantly meditate (literally, to "mutter, talk to one's self, ponder") on the wonders He has done.

When we forget His faithfulness, our spiritual senses become dull. One day Jesus, while teaching His disciples, mentioned the word *yeast* in an illustration. Although the disciples had just participated in an amazing feeding of 5,000 men from a young boy's small lunch, they began to be afraid. They feared that Jesus was giving them a subtle hint that once again they had run out of bread. Jesus wasted no time in firmly rebuking them. He asked, "Do you have eyes, but fail to see, and ears but fail to hear?" They had lost the capacity to spiritually *see* and *hear* what the Lord was doing. He went on to say, "And don't you remember?" (See Mark 8:17.) They could not see what God was doing because they forgot what He had done.

Remembering His goodness awakens our spiritual sensitivity.

Ask the Holy Spirit to remind you of specific incidents in which you experienced the faithfulness of the Lord.

What does He show you?

As you join with the Holy Spirit in remembering, ask the Holy Spirit to open your eyes to all the Lord wants to show you.

What do you see? What do you hear?

CHAPTER 8

His Healing Presence

The battle is the Lord's
(1 Samuel 17:47b).

All during this trial, the outpouring of support proved overwhelming. Several women helped Sheri clean the house each week, and meals arrived every weekday. In fact, food was given in such abundance that each weekend the children could feast on a smorgasbord of leftovers. Ben, our older son, didn't realize that the church was continuing to support us financially. Taking his "man of the house" role seriously, he would regularly try to motivate his picky eater little brother. When Brandon wrinkled his nose at some new and unusual casserole, Ben advised, "You'd better eat, Brandon, because this is all you're getting. Now that Dad can't work, we don't have any money. So people are bringing us food." Ben also informed his mother that he was prepared to drop out of the sixth grade so he could go to work to support the family. While Sheri immediately reassured Ben that we had enough money, she was touched by his desire to make any sacrifice to help his family through the difficult season.

The greatest gift we received was the time others spent in the presence of the Lord praying for us. Because people so often say, "We felt your prayers," the statement may sound cliché. But—we *felt* their prayers. Our hearts were strengthened and demonic attacks were thwarted because people chose to believe in faith that God would meet our needs. Only eternity will reveal the depth and scope of the impact made by these people praying for us in Jesus' name. Jesus' brother James put it so well: "You do not have because you do not ask" (James 4:2). They asked. And we had. Heavenly resources flooded our hearts.

Because of my weakened immune system, I was quarantined to my room. At times it seemed like a prison cell, minus the barred windows. Visits were limited to family members who had to wear gowns and masks while I was undergoing treatment. Dressed like hazardous material workers, they were within reach, yet I was unable to touch them. I wondered if God ever felt this way. Frustrated. Longing to draw us close, while we stood just beyond His outstretched arms.

My room was situated at an angle, allowing me to look out of my window into the visitors' room around the corner on my floor. Often in the very early hours of the morning, I would pace in my room with Matilda in tow, praying for family, friends, and people in our region. Frequently I would gaze across to the visitors' room and see the faces of friends who had come during the night to pray for me. Some would place their hands on the window and smile. I would do the same. Though 50 yards apart, our hearts connected.

We were tasting the unity of the Spirit, experiencing what it means to be joined together as "members of one another"

(Eph. 4:25 KJV). Far more than being fellow members of an organization, we were truly united in His presence.

One of our friends regularly drove his car around the hospital praying "Joshua-versus-Jericho" prayers on my behalf, taking authority over the "walls" of cancer. My mother, a cancer survivor herself, daily cried out for God's healing presence to flood my body. Others sent prayers and words of encouragement via e-mail. We heard reports of spontaneous gatherings in lunchrooms and living rooms to agree in prayer.

Space does not allow me to thank all of those who stood with us in this time of need. I am convinced their prayers shook the heavens and changed things here on earth, not because of the amount of people praying, but because of the fervency in their hearts. As James said, "The earnest (heartfelt, continued) prayer of a righteous man makes tremendous power available [dynamic in its working]" (James 5:16b AMP). Never believe for a moment that unless half a city prays, things will not change. Abraham cried out to the Lord on behalf of the city of Sodom, and its judgment was postponed (see Gen. 18). Moses prayed, and the destruction of the Israelites was averted (see Exod. 32). One man's prayers saved a city. Another man's prayers saved an entire nation. Truly the prayer of one righteous person "makes tremendous power available—dynamic in its working!" If you have just one godly person praying for you in Jesus' name, tremendous power is being released into your situation right now!

My parents dropped by faithfully. They would usually smuggle food, hidden behind one of my mother's "suitcase" purses. After witnessing only one of my adverse facial reactions to the hospital food, my mother's protective instincts kicked into high gear. She and Dad were on a mission where no mountain was high enough to keep them from procuring me food. Poker-faced, they would sneak past the nurses' station with concealed nourishment. For them, it was the height of espionage, providing an adrenaline rush each time they would successfully sashay past the head nurse. Their covert "feeding program" was a highlight of each week.

The word *manna*—the miracle bread in the wilderness— means, "What is it?" I frequently had "manna" experiences with the hospital meals on my dinner tray. One particular "manna-fold" evening brought an unknown casserole, which looked like a zucchini had collided with a pork product! "You're not eating that!" my father declared, while snatching my plate and retreating into the bathroom. With the noise of the receding waters in the background, he stepped back into the room and found himself face-to-face with one of the nuns assigned to my floor. Empty dinner plate in hand, guilt flooded his cheeks. Feeling like a schoolboy caught red-handed, he smiled sheepishly and said, "Boy, that was good!" Sister Paula blessed him and left the room. And then we laughed.

We needed to laugh.

Dad was a sales representative for a cabinet company, covering the Mid-Atlantic states. Many times after a long day of travel, he would "happen" to stop by on his way home. Through heavy eyelids I would see him early in the morning, sleeping in the chair at the foot of my bed. Childhood memories came rushing back in those moments, reminding me of my parents' watchful care in those early years of our lives. Often Dad would tearfully exclaim, "If I could trade places with you right now, I would." I understood. I thought of my own young children and how I would feel if their lives were threatened. I guess you never stop being a father.

It made me think of my heavenly Father. His heart so throbs with love for us that He went to ultimate lengths to draw us into His world. Sacrificing His own Son's life, He unloaded Heaven itself for us. Right now He is wrapped up in the midst of your situation. And He is able to do far beyond all you could ask or imagine!

As time ticked on, I found myself missing many things. Toward the top of my list was my piano. Through the years, playing and singing to the Lord provided an instant tabernacle where my heart would meet with His. Through persistence, I eventually convinced Rosemary and Sister Paula to accompany me to the chapel for "therapy" time. With official approval, we would occasionally make the trek to the main floor after visiting hours. There, where the scent of aged hardwood, candle wax, and old hymnals mingled, I would sit at the piano and worship Him. I often sang:

> When I look into Your holiness;
> when I gaze into Your loveliness;
> When all things that surround become shadows
> in the light of You....[1]

The presence of the Lord seemed to envelop us in those moments. He put all things in perspective. All things, including cancer, became a shadow in the light of His presence.

Just before I commenced with the next seven-day round of chemotherapy, my younger brother and sister submitted blood tests to see if they could be bone marrow donors for my transplant. Both Daniel and Lori told me that they would do anything they could to save my life. Their eager willingness to undergo this very tedious procedure touched me. Words cannot express how deeply moved I was by their surrendered acts of love.

We had always been close, growing up together, despite the difference in ages—Lori being five years younger and Daniel coming along three years after her. Because of the age gaps, I was the undisputed "big brother." Perhaps my earliest desire to become a pastor grew from my habit of keeping an eye on them. Protecting them. Instructing them. Even as an adult, I made weekly calls, checking to make sure they were all right. I felt a God-given responsibility to watch over them.

And now they were watching over me.

Lori married a wise and wonderful young man from our home church, who later became a lawyer. She became an accomplished harpist and a mother. They moved to a small farm where they were raising two fine sons, a precious daughter, and a set of golden retrievers.

Daniel married his childhood sweetheart. He is a gifted history teacher at a local high school. He is also a skilled piano player and worship leader, not to mention the wildest, craziest, most uninhibited funny man you would ever want to meet. His wife Beth knows how to handle him though. Together they had three daughters...and a lot of bathrooms.

The test results confirmed that Daniel's bone marrow type was a near-perfect match with mine. Arrangements were made for Sheri and me to meet with a transplant specialist at a large regional hospital to discuss plans for the procedure. Because Sheri's sister Robin was trained as a registered nurse, she and her husband Bob graciously agreed to accompany us to the consultation. We needed Robin's medical wisdom to translate the medical phraseology into terms we could understand. Very simple terms.

Ushered into the office of a young physician, hurried introductions were followed by a recounting of the hospital's impressive success rate with bone marrow transplants. Then he explained that the transplant unit does not automatically treat every patient who applies simply because they have a matching donor. Puzzled, we asked him about his review of our specific case. *Could I receive a bone marrow transplant?*

He responded, "Your leukemia is very aggressive. You apparently had the disease for a significant amount of time before your diagnosis and initial treatment." Glancing at my medical record, he continued bluntly, "You are a high risk for the probability of a successful transplant. So, to answer your question—no, we do not believe you would be a good candidate for a bone marrow transplant. I recommend you continue with your chemotherapy regimen and see how things turn out."

Robin asked him a barrage of questions, to which he gave the same answer: "No!" They spoke "medical-ese" for a few minutes longer, until he gave the "I've-got-a-lot-to-do-and-a-short-time-to-get-it-done" look and handed my sizeable paperwork back to me.

Standing up quickly behind the desk, he extended his hand to me and said, "Mr. Hess, I wish you the best." With a nervous smile and a hurried glance at his watch, he showed us to the door.

We walked out of his office and through the large cancer unit. The hallways were lined with cancer patients. Their hopeless stares, coupled with either obvious marks or more subtle signs of the disease, created an atmosphere of despair. *How I hate cancer!* I inwardly exclaimed. I resolved afresh to use every Spirit-born weapon and every natural means possible to eradicate the disease! *Lord, let Your Kingdom come to this part of the planet! Let Heaven fill this corner of the world! Establish a "cancer-free zone" right here on the earth!* This cry erupted in my soul. And its molten ferocity remains to this day.

We stepped outside into the chilly January air, stunned by what we had just heard.

"No wonder they have such a great track record!" Sheri fumed. The frustration she had corked in the doctor's office was about to pop. "They only take the 'guaranteed to succeed' patients!" she blurted, her sense of justice violated. "What about the rest of the people? What are they to do?"

She then looked at me, showing the first visible signs that this journey was shaking her. "What are *we* to do?"

In all our years together, I have never wondered what my wife was thinking. She aimed straight, lived straight, and spoke straight. At this moment I fully understood her feelings and shared her frustration.

After emoting for a bit, we felt as if the Holy Spirit said, "Now that you've gotten that out of your system, let Me remind you of the promises I made to you:

- ❖ "You will not die, but live.

- ❖ You will declare what the Lord has done, because...

- ❖ This battle is the Lord's,

- ❖ And He has opened a door of hope for you in your valley of trouble."

With a splash of His living water, we snapped back to our senses. The cancer was real. But Jesus is the Truth. We were not victims of hospital politics. We were more than conquerors in His Kingdom, children of the Great Physician! As much as we wanted a healing, we needed Him — the Healer. And He was healing us right now of bitterness and despair. More than simply touching my body with His healing power, He was saturating my entire life with His healing presence.

With fresh resolve, we returned to Holy Spirit Hospital for round two of chemotherapy.

This was about to be a new test of our faith.

ENDNOTE

1. Cathy Perrin and Wayne Perrin, "When I Look Into Your Holiness."

My Personal Journal of Hope

I am constantly baffled at our reluctance to ask the Lord to help us. With so many clear challenges in the Bible to make our requests known and to keep asking, seeking, and knocking, we have no right to foolishly attempt to live in self-sufficiency.

The fact of the matter is: We need Him. We were not created to live without Him. He hears the desperate cry of our hearts and responds with His abundant supply.

Psalm 42:1 states, "As the deer pants for streams of water, so my soul pants for You, O God." God responds with much more than a small stream of water. Instead, His "waterfalls" and "waves and breakers" sweep over us as we cry out for more (Ps. 42:7).

What help do you require from the Lord at this moment in your life?

_____

_____

_____

_____

HOPE BEYOND REASON

What does your body cry out for at this point in time?

What are your mental and emotional needs?

What is your greatest spiritual hunger?

_____

_____

_____

_____

_____

_____

_____

HOPE BEYOND REASON

CHAPTER 9

Walking Through Affliction

Even though I walk through the valley
of the shadow of death, I will fear
no evil, for You are with me
(Psalm 23:4a).

The second round of chemotherapy seemed to be going smoothly. All through the day and night, shifts of nursing staff would sweep through my room. Changing I.V. bags, checking the tubes, and programming the machinery, they would chat with me about the weather, their children, and anything else happening in their world. Matilda forgave my brief absence and returned as my waltzing partner, churning steadily as liquids flowed through the rubber tubes into my chest.

Rosemary, my nurse, was asking more questions about the Bible. I watched as her stern countenance melted into warm smiles. (And to think, she had once hated preachers!) When she overheard me humming a chorus one day, she asked me to teach it to her. Rosemary said she didn't know many hymns, choruses, or other "religious stuff like that." Soon after, I discovered that we were both fans of Louis Armstrong. We had found a happy meeting ground! We would often sing "What a Wonderful World," changing the last line of the song to "...I say to myself, what a wonderful God!"

Holy Spirit Hospital operates under the supervision of the Roman Catholic Church. That partnership fosters a special atmosphere in the place. Scripture readings and prayer begin and end each day over the P.A. system, with various staff members sharing their thoughts about a passage of the Bible. Then they pray for the staff and patients. At times the practice seemed tedious and religious. Yet on other days, their words were rivers of life.

During my stay, I met and spent more time talking with nuns than I ever had in my life. In fact, prior to this time, I did not remember ever speaking with a nun. Sadly, the only exposure I had were the sisters I had seen in *The Sound of Music.*

Now I had the privilege of spending time with several of them—and especially with Sister Paula Marie. For many years she had covered this cancer ward. Roaming the hallways with a cart filled with inspirational books, she would weave in and out of our rooms sharing her kind eyes and gracious words with us. She called us *her* patients, caring for us less like a sister, and more like a mother. She was a devoted lover of Jesus Christ and a gifted poet. She would stop by and read her poems, predominantly prayers written in verse. A lover of the Bible, she would read chapters to me on days when I was very weak. I would close my eyes and let the words sink deep into my spirit.

She would pray over me with words written in a prayer book and then ask me to pray for her. I didn't use a prayer book. Not having grown up in that tradition, I simply prayed spontaneously for her from my heart.

One day she asked, "How do you do that? How do you just pray off the top of your head?"

"There's nothing wrong with written prayers, if they're good ones," I responded. "You know when you buy a greeting card," I continued, "and they have nice, lyrical verses written inside? That's what written prayers are like. While I enjoy receiving cards and reading those poems, my favorite part is reading the words people write at the bottom. Praying written prayers is great. But don't forget to write something at the bottom of the card that comes from *your* heart. Jesus likes that!"

Sister Paula smiled and thanked me. From time to time she would pop her head into my room and say, "I'm writing at the bottom of the card, Reverend Hess!" She always called me *reverend*. She's the *only* person who has ever called me that.

And I always called her "sister." On the final day of the second round of chemotherapy, they removed the I.V. bags and pulled the tubes. Dr. King's exclamation, "Free at last!" rose up in my soul. *Free!* I was able to move about, divorced from Matilda for a few hours. When the tubes came off, I usually took a victory lap through the hallways, celebrating my liberty. Early in the morning, they would allow me to leave my room. It was before visiting hours...and more people...and fresh germs.

The simple act of carrying my Bible while walking to the visitors' room—without an I.V. apparatus tagging along—made me feel somewhat human again. I plopped down into a plastic, leather-looking, foam-filled chair in the corner. Although it was not the most comfortable chair I ever sat in, it was really good to be out of my bed.

I paged to a chapter of Isaiah and began to feed my soul.

Within a few moments, a few other patients shuffled into the room. Some had poles. Others did not. All of them looked drained. I glanced up to smile at each of them and then turned back to Isaiah.

For I the Lord your God hold your right hand; I am the Lord, Who says to you, Fear not; I will help you! (Isaiah 41:13 AMP).

These words leaped into my spirit, stirring me to trust Him more.

In my peripheral view, I noticed one of the men in the room staring at me. Glancing up, I caught his quizzical gaze.

"So what are you readin'?" he asked, slowly rising from his chair and moving toward me with staggered steps.

"Some really good stuff," I answered. "Do you want to hear it?"

"Go right ahead," he said. "I got nothing better to do."

I read the verse out loud to him: "Fear not! I will help you!"

"Do you believe that?" he asked me, with a look that seemed to say he hoped it was true.

I told him I did. And I told him why. Without preaching, I talked about my very real fears at this moment in my life. I also talked about Jesus' very real presence with me at times like these.

Recently diagnosed with chronic leukemia and fearful for his life, he questioned, "Do you think *He* can help you?"

I nodded. "And He can help you, too," I said, compassion for him rising in my heart. "Can I pray for you?" I offered, an expectant expression appearing on my face.

He nodded.

Closing my Bible, I placed my hand on a small patch of the remaining hair on his head. He leaned forward, making the sign of the cross. I prayed a simple prayer that went straight to the point: I asked the Father to heal his body, and I asked Jesus to draw him near to His heart.

We both wiped away some tears. Unable to talk, he mouthed the words, "Thank you," and slowly maneuvered toward the door. I told him I would continue to pray for him. He waved without turning around and hobbled out the door. As he left, I wondered if I would see him again. It took a few weeks until I had my answer. One morning he and his wife came to the door of my room. Dressed in street clothes and wearing a broad smile, he blurted, "No more cancer. I'm going home!" As he turned to go, he looked back and said, "Thanks for praying for me. It really helped."

In the visitors' room I finished reading Isaiah. Closing my eyes, I silently soaked in the Lord's love for me. He filled me with it. New mercy. Fresh every morning. I became so lost in His presence that I momentarily forgot where I was. Then the loudspeaker lady, paging another doctor, reminded me. I remembered that I would hear the initial reports about my white cell count the next morning. After a brief shuffle around the room and a stroll down the hallway, I returned to my bed and quickly fell into a deep sleep.

In fact, I slept most of that day. People were in and out of my room, yet I was too exhausted to interact with them. I heard them through a haze of drowsiness, but they seemed to be miles away. I heard the squeaking of nurses' shoes. Visitors whispered, "I think he's asleep." My dinner tray was placed on my bedside table and then carried away again, untouched. I clawed and crawled inside my head, trying to escape sleep, only to slip back into it once again.

During the early hours of the morning, I awoke with a start. A phrase had been impressed upon my mind as I slept. Creeping toward consciousness, the phrase grew stronger. There it was again! *Nahum 1:9! Nahum 1:9!* Repeated over and over.

Turning on the light beside my bed, I slid my Bible onto my lap and paged to the Old Testament book written by the prophet Nahum. Nahum 1:9 didn't ring a bell in my memory bank. Flipping the pages, I thought, "Here I am in the middle of the night looking up an obscure verse in the Old Testament." With a hint of sarcasm, I said out loud, "It's probably a long list of people whose names I can't pronounce! Or the account of an obscure king getting hemorrhoids!"

But to my surprise, I read these words:

Affliction will not rise up a second time (Nahum 1:9b NKJV).

I wasn't sure what this meant. But like Mary the mother of Jesus, I tucked it into my heart to ponder through the night. Though I didn't have full understanding, I knew that Jesus was speaking to me. "Do not refuse Him who is speaking," we are warned (Heb. 12:25 NASB). He has not stopped speaking to us. Too often, we have stopped listening.

The next morning I was greeted by one of the oncologists. He seemed fairly pleased with my results, which showed that healthy white cells were being produced in my body once again. At this point, not a trace of blast cells could be found. *Yea, God!*

Turning to leave, he informed me that I would need both blood and platelet transfusions. Then he continued, "Although this is a good report, I don't want you to think that you're out of the woods yet. Acute leukemia is very aggressive. It can, in some cases, *rise up a second time,* even stronger than it did at first."

I had heard that phrase before! *"Rise up a second time!"* And yet, the Great Physician whom I had heard it from during the night said, "Affliction will not rise up a second time!" He gave me His "second opinion" first!

Sometimes God's words to us explain what has already happened. At other times they prepare us for what is going to happen. In this case, His words shielded me from the enemy's sneak attack of fear. It caused me to realize afresh the importance of hearing His voice.

I did not fully comprehend, until the events of the next few weeks transpired, how much I would need to hold onto His promises in my heart. While He opens the door of hope, we have a responsibility to walk through it. Even run through it! Solomon reminds us that the Lord is our place of refuge in the fiercest of battles. He draws near to us. But we must respond to Him. He says, "The name [that is, the authority and character] of the Lord is a strong tower; the righteous run to it and are safe" (Prov. 18:10).

Some things He brings to us as soon as we utter our first prayer. We ask, and He brings an immediate, effortless answer. So spontaneous is His reply, we imagine that all of life will be like this. Easy. As if we have discovered a secret formula for instant answers from God.

Yet other times are nothing like that. There are hard times when we face difficulties, filled with only delays and deafening silence. In these times He calls us to run the race, not giving in to weariness. We must fight the good fight. Stand our ground. Press on. And press in. It is in these moments we discover that "He *is* [He definitely exists], and that He is a rewarder of those who *diligently* seek Him" (Heb. 11:6b NKJV).

This doesn't mean that we enjoy His provision in the easy times while relying on our own strength in the hard times. Nothing could be farther from the truth. While called to do our part, we never do it alone. Paul described it well with these words: *"I labor* [I do *my* part], struggling with all *His energy* [God's supply], which so powerfully works in me" (Col. 1:29). We were moving into a time that would increase the demands on Sheri and me. But we were about to discover deeper reservoirs of the Lord's strength. Deeper than we have ever known.

The next season was a haze to me. My body reacted violently to the platelet transfusions. Delirious from high fevers, I spent many hours lying on the cooling blanket, shivering and burning up. Covers on. Then covers off. There seemed to be no relief. I ate very little, having lost all desire for food—even Chinese food and Rice Krispies!

Sheri, the children, and other family members came to see me, but I felt semi-oblivious to their presence. Though I tried to focus, it was extremely difficult. In my weakened state, I contracted an infection that led to pneumonia. All I could do was lie there. Wait. And trust.

Yet in all of this, the presence of the Lord would come to me in waves. One wave might be more powerful than another, but I was experiencing His presence with me. I didn't talk to Him much, feeling free to simply *receive* from Him. At times like these, I realized how important it is to hide His Word in my heart. I thought of Jesus' story of the ten virgins (see Matt. 25:1-3). Five of them kept their lamps filled with oil. The other five allowed their supply to run out, carelessly believing they had plenty of time to prepare. Yet when the required hour came upon them without warning, the five with filled lamps walked into the moment, their lamps burning brightly. The other five scrambled in vain to make up for days of neglect. Sadly, they realized that their time had come and gone. And they were not prepared.

There in my hospital bed, almost too weak to breathe, I began to open jars of oil stored in previous seasons. I could not physically open my Bible, turn on a tape, or even sing a song. But, like forest creatures emerging in the night, His words and thoughts and songs and testimonies came to me in these dark moments, soothing my soul. "Times of refreshing" truly "come from the Lord" (Acts 3:19).

Then it all broke. Fever, nausea, chills, difficulty breathing—everything seemed to leave me like unwanted telemarketers who finally understood the words "Not interested." Relieved but exhausted, I was discharged to home for a few days before the final round of chemo. Barely had I unpacked my suitcase before I was filling it again.

Within a few days I returned to the hospital, feeling like a bowling pin being set up for the next frame. By this time, I knew the routine. Seven days of absorbing multiple I.V. bags of various colored liquids, followed by a few blood transfusions.

And then, home.

What a delightful thought! What a goal! These months had already seemed like years. How I missed my wife. And the children. And the church. Yes, I even missed our dog Harry.

One afternoon during my third round of chemo, I had one of those Kodak-moment surprises I will treasure forever. Our daughter Bethany was going to her high school prom with one of the young men from our church.

"We have a surprise for you." Sheri beamed from the door.

Bethany stepped around the corner, looking like a princess. Her beautifully manicured hair decorated her face, curls and swirls dancing in synchronized layers. Her eyes sparkled in coordination with her gown, which shimmered in the fluorescent light.

"I wanted you to have the first dance, Daddy," she said. "But don't make me cry. It'll mess up my makeup."

I waltzed with Matilda over to Bethany's side, and we danced. It was kind of like a swaying hug. I softly sang Joe Cocker's song, "You Are So Beautiful," gravelly voice and all, meaning every word. For a moment, I was back in time, holding the hands of my three-year-old girl who would stand on the tops of my shoes as we danced at Cinderella's ball.

Following the final round of chemo, I received another series of platelet transfusions that sent my body off the deep end. Various infections began to attack my struggling immune system. I returned to the cooling blanket once again as my fever spiked higher than it had ever gone. Oxygen tubes were placed in my nose to assist my labored breathing. As my fever soared above the 105-degree mark, I blacked out.

Rosemary stood with Sheri at my bedside. With an ashen look on her face, she squeezed Sheri's hand and said, "This may be it! This is often how they go!"

Sheri stepped out of the room to notify friends and family once again. Within moments, a company of prayer warriors would press into this battle with us. I was later told that while Sheri was out of the room, medical staff worked at one point to revive me. They clearly thought I was gone.

Yet I was oblivious to all of this.

Unaware of my body, I became keenly aware that I was standing in the presence of Jesus. He was obscured from clear view by a translucent cloud surrounding Him. Though it screened me from glimpsing His face, everything inside of me wanted to see Him. To be with Him. It was the most intense magnetic pull I have ever experienced. His presence was so overwhelmingly attractive that everything within me wanted to plunge into Him. It was the most peaceful place I have ever been. I lingered with Him in timeless pleasure.

And then, it was almost as if a black curtain descended, obscuring my sight of Him. My eyes began to open, and through a dissipating haze I recognized Sheri's face. We were alone in the room. Several hours had passed, and outside my window the day was fading.

Sheri looked exhausted. Tearfully, she recounted the trauma she had witnessed. Nurses streaming into the room. Alarming noises coming from ominous medical equipment. A concerned huddle of medical personnel fighting to regulate my stalling heart. But it was over now. She held me and sobbed, "I thought I was losing you." We embraced for a long time. It was good to hold her again, without antibacterial gowns, masks, or precautionary signs warning people not to touch me.

Then I told her where I had been.

"Going home to be with Him will be wonderful," I said, knowing I could never adequately describe what I had seen. "But I'd like to stick around for a while."

She smiled.

With a sudden impulse, I blurted, "Help me get out of bed."

"What? You almost died. You're not supposed to do that."

"Just for a moment," I begged. "Help me move this bed rail out of the way."

Reluctantly, Sheri went along with my plan. "Why are we doing this?" she pleaded one last time.

"I think we're supposed to stand," I explained. "I just heard one word in my spirit. Jesus said: '*Stand!*'"

Wobbly-legged and bleary-eyed, I managed to move from the bed to the middle of the room. There we stood: Sheri on one side, Matilda on the other.

Standing.

I began to speak and Sheri joined me. We declared every promise the Lord had given us up to that point: "I will not die. I will live. And I will declare what the Lord has done! This affliction will not rise up a second time! He will take us through this dark corridor, and when we come out the other side, we will strengthen others! In this valley of trouble, He has opened a door of hope!"

When we sensed that we were finished, Sheri helped me back into bed. Tucking me in, she gave me a look that said, "Don't scare me like that again!"

I smiled as if to say, "I'll try not to."

As she slipped out the door, I lay back on my pillow, grateful to be alive.

My Personal Journal of Hope

Give ear and come to Me; hear Me, that your soul may live (Isaiah 55:3).

The Lord is the best communicator around. And He has a lot to say to you. He speaks to you daily through every means possible. A passing thought. An open vision. A timely dream. The word of a friend. A natural event that is filled with supernatural revelations. All of these and more serve to speak life to our souls and hope to our hearts.

What has He been saying to you lately?

_____

_____

_____

_____

_____

_____

His words bring change. In the beginning, His declaration of "Let there be light" terminated the darkness (Gen. 1:3). "He sent forth His word and healed them" (Ps. 107:20). Jesus drove demons from oppressed people "with a word, and healed all the sick" (Matt. 8:16).

What effects are His words having on your life right now?

HOPE BEYOND REASON

CHAPTER 10

A Shield Around Me

No weapon forged
against you will prevail
(Isaiah 54:17a).

Three days later I was awakened in the night with intense abdominal pain. My appetite had begun to improve, so I had eaten some broccoli earlier that day. It was the first significant amount of food I had eaten for quite some time. As the discomfort in my lower tract increased, I thought I might simply be suffering the results of my dinner.

My high school track coach had taught us that the best way to relieve gastrointestinal pain was to do the "bicycle exercise," rolling up on your shoulders while pedaling in the air. So I tried it. Hospital beds and designer hospital gowns were definitely not made for such an activity. But I was in a private room, praying that no nurse would come through the door at that moment.

When bicycling didn't improve things, I tried walking up and down the hallways. It seemed to work for the older men who paced the corridors in the morning. It was about 4:00 A.M. The nurses at the station wondered what I was doing up so early, so I explained. (I like nurses. You can talk to them about things like intestinal gas without feeling embarrassed.)

As morning light beamed through my window, the pain in my abdomen escalated. Within a few hours, it was almost unbearable. One of my doctors examined me. His scowl told me something was wrong. A series of X-rays were taken, and their worst fears were realized.

My appendix had ruptured during the night. The problem? I was inoperable.

Chemotherapy is cumulative. Each round builds upon the previous regimen. By my third series of seven-day chemo treatments, it was as if I was receiving the effects of all three of them—at one time.

At this point, my white cells were depleted, greatly reducing my ability to fight infection. Even worse, my platelet count was low, keeping my blood from clotting. An operation at this point in time was completely out of the question. In plain words, I would not be able to survive any surgical procedure. In my current condition, I would contract infections while bleeding to death on the operating table. And without an operation, the poison released from a ruptured appendix is fatal.

The doctors called Sheri. She was at one of the boys' soccer games, cheering them on as usual. The physician told her to get to the hospital immediately, saying it might be the last time she would see me alive.

After over four months on this roller coaster ride, Sheri was emotionally drained. She scrambled to organize the unfolding chaos, asking one of our friends to take the children home after the game. Trying not to alarm our kids, she simply said, "I have to go to the hospital to check on a few things."

When she arrived, she was greeted by a physician who gravely told her, "Mrs. Hess, I am so sorry. Your husband seems like such a nice guy. We hate to see it end this way."

But one of the doctors was not willing to give up and suggested one more option. He found a surgeon who was willing to attempt inserting a tube through my abdominal wall to drain some of the fluid. To do this, however, I would need a platelet transfusion first.

Following the platelet procedure, I was rushed to the operating room. There, while I was wide awake, the operation began. Sparing the details, I will simply say that it was one of the most painful experiences I have ever had. On top of this, I had another intense reaction to the platelet transfusion. The combination of the pain and the high fever finally overwhelmed me. I passed out on the table, unsure of where I would wake up.

Meanwhile, another battalion of prayer warriors was converging at the church, joining together to fight for us. Sheri kept them updated by phone. Others arrived at the hospital to stand with her.

Hours later I was back in my room. One of the nurses told me that the tube had been successfully inserted after numerous attempts. "This might control some of the poison," she stated, "but it will not take care of the damaged appendix."

At this point we were given the most sobering news we heard at any time in this ordeal. "It will take weeks for your blood levels to rise to an operable level," the physician stated, almost choking on his words, "and we do not have that kind of time. In all of my research, I have not found a case where an adult has survived with a ruptured appendix for more than a few days. There are two cases where two little boys in England survived for a few weeks. They were taking heavy doses of antibiotics to sustain them until they could face surgery.

"We'll try the antibiotic route. But my prognosis is that you'll have about two or three more days to live. We'll keep you comfortable until then." He could say no more. He hugged us both and walked out the door.

And we walked through the door of hope.

The next morning, another physician came to my room. He slowly closed the door behind him and paused, appearing to have something to say. It was clearly something he had thought about for a while but was unsure of how to say it.

Moving toward my bed, he tossed my medical chart onto the bedside table, almost as if to discard it. "Mr. Hess," he began, "we have done everything we can. There is no more for us to do."

With greater urgency than I had ever seen on his face, he advised, "Pray to your God. Pray to *your* God. He is your only hope." In prior dialogue, he had expressed to me that he believed there were many roads to God. Now, his assumptions seemed to be shaken.

In light of our previous discussions, I gently asked him, "Who is my God? What is His name?"

Straightening up, he said without flinching, "His name is Jesus Christ. And in all my years of practice, I have seen miracles happen when people call on His name."

So we continued to call on Jesus' name.

At this point I recalled an event that had happened two weeks prior to my appendix rupturing. One afternoon, Charles and Anne Stock, pastors of Life Center Ministries in Harrisburg, stopped by to pray with us. They brought with them their friend Randy Clark, a Vineyard pastor instrumental in the Toronto outpouring. Sheri and I had never met Randy, but we quickly took to his down-home demeanor and unshakeable faith. With a gentle smile, Randy told us stories of miracles he had seen Jesus do in recent days. The faith climate in my heart increased with each testimony. After a while, this trio of friends began to pray for us. Simple, yet passionate cries filled the room as we honored Jesus for who He is and thanked Him for what He was doing. At one point I felt a burning sensation in the middle of my forehead. It wasn't painful, but it was persistent, seeming to move in a swirling motion.

As the fervency of prayer came to a lull, Randy asked me if I was feeling anything in my body. Reporting the fire on my forehead, he told us of various incidents where people being healed of blood disorders and cancers recalled similar sensations. We continued to pray, thanking Jesus once again for what He was doing in my body.

When the fire subsided, Randy held his hand about a foot or so above my abdominal area. In his unassuming style, he said, "I'm not sure why I'm praying for your abdominal area, but I believe that the Lord is doing a healing work there, too." At the time, I had no discomfort in that part of my body. Yet sensing the Lord's direction, we continued to pray.

Now two weeks later, facing a medical crisis in my abdominal region, I recalled Randy's prayer. Though he did not understand why at the time, he had stepped out in faith. He went with a nudge from the Father, taking a risk. And I was glad he did. Between waves of pain that coursed through my midsection, I continued to bless what the Lord was doing to heal my appendix. In sporadic coherent moments, I thanked the Lord for people like Randy who model obedient faith. I resolved to spend my days stepping out of my comfort zones. We weren't made to lean on our own understanding. We were created to trust in the Lord with all our hearts. Trust is the atmosphere of His Kingdom, the safest place to take a risk.

Over the next two days, I met with our children. I purposely did not make things morbid or melodramatic. I listened to their questions and answered them as best I could. As they left at the end of the second day, I laid my hands on their heads and blessed them. I prayed my deepest desires for their lives, asking the Father to let all Heaven break loose upon them as they fulfilled their destinies. I prayed as if it were the last time I would have a chance to do so.

Then Sheri prayed for me. It was a prayer similar to the one she expressed at the beginning of this journey. As they left, I watched her and the children from my window, following them with my eyes until their car disappeared from my sight.

Then I gingerly lowered myself into bed.

As I awoke the next morning, I stared up at the same water-stained ceiling tiles I had been looking at each morning for months. *They don't have ceiling tiles in Heaven!* I thought. To my alarm, one of the nuns had slipped into my room. She had a cheerful face, stood about four-and-a-half feet tall, and was dressed in an all-white habit. She frightened me for a moment! *Is this Gabriel? I always thought he would be taller!*

But...*I wasn't in Heaven! I was still here! No streets of gold and giant, adoring angels. Just stained ceiling tiles and a short nun!*

One of the older women from our church had shared a word with me. I remembered it now, and it seemed timely. "I'm not sure what this means, but you will find the Lord to be a shield around you. ...I know that's in the Bible somewhere, or maybe in a song." She continued with matter-of-fact certainty, "I just know He wanted you to know that." I later found this phrase in one of David's psalms. He wrote: "You are a shield around me, O Lord" (Ps. 3:3).

Lying in my bed, I repeated the phrase out loud several times. Peace settled into my soul. And fear took flight.

Two more weeks passed, much to the amazement of the medical team. I didn't seem to be dying at the rate they thought I would. One of the social workers talked with me about hospice care. She said they would take good care of me in my final days at home and help me to manage my pain as I faced death. I appreciated the willingness of hospice workers to serve people in this way. *What a labor of love,* I thought. But I wasn't planning to need their care at this time.

I wasn't afraid of dying; I looked forward to seeing Jesus face-to-face. I just didn't want to die right now.

Eventually I was sent home, without hospice care, to wait for my blood levels to return to an operable level. I checked in with the doctor every other day to have my blood tested. The moment the levels rose to an operable range, they would take a look inside me. They were curious to know what was going on in there. Why was I still alive? I was curious, too.

Finally, after six weeks, my blood levels were restored. With white cells, red cells, and platelets in healthy balance, I met with the surgeon to prepare for surgery.

"I've looked over your charts," he said. "You've had a ruptured appendix inside you for over six weeks. I'm going to do an exploratory procedure on you because I'm not sure what we will find. The poison that is secreted from a burst appendix is highly toxic. We need to see what damage has been done to your internal organs."

Grateful to be alive, I underwent surgery the next morning. As I nodded off, counting backwards at the direction of the anesthetist, I remembered Jesus' promise to me. *You are a shield around me,* I said to Him as I drifted off into an anesthetic fog.

Later in the recovery room, the surgeon greeted Sheri and me. His first words to us were exclamations of amazement: "I've never seen anything like this!" Holding up four snapshots, he said, "Look at these pictures!"

They were pictures of my insides in 5x7 glossy prints. *Suitable for framing.*

"Here," he said, pointing at one of the photos, "is your appendix, or what is left of it. Amazingly, it is encased inside a tent-like structure that completely encompasses your appendix! Did you ever have an operation in this part of your body?" he asked.

"Not that I remember," I responded. "Why do you ask?"

"Because this tent is composed of adhesions. It's the strongest type of scar tissue your body can manufacture. This kind of scar tissue only appears *after* someone has had surgery! It appears to have been in place *before* your appendix ruptured. All of the poison was contained inside it," he said, while making a circular gesture on the photo. "Not a drop of poison escaped this tent. Your entire internal system is as healthy as that of a 20-year-old!" *What a compliment!* I thought.

Bewildered, relieved, grateful, and amazed, I asked him, "What did this tent of adhesions look like?"

"That's the funniest thing," he said curiously. "It looked like a group of shields that had been sewn together!"

Just as He promised, so He had done. The Lord had miraculously created a miracle pouch. A tent of shields. Grabbing my Bible, I opened once again to the passage containing His timely word to us. I marvel at it to this day.

> *Many are saying of me, "God will not deliver him." But You are a shield around me, O Lord* (Psalm 3:2-3).

Just when we thought we had come to the end, He opened the door to a new beginning. In the darkest moment in our valley of trouble, He opened a gateway of Hope!

My Personal Journal of Hope

There is a powerful chain reaction going on inside of you. In spite of the difficult moments you are facing, God is at work in you. Through Him we can "rejoice in our sufferings, because we know that suffering produces *perseverance*; perseverance, *character*; and character, *hope*" (Rom. 5:3-4).

Although traumatic experiences seem determined to wear us down, our Father is devoted to build us up.

What is He actively working into your heart right now?

_____

_____

_____

_____

_____

_____

Romans 5:5 continues: "*And hope does not disappoint us*, because God has poured out His love into our hearts by the Holy Spirit, whom He has given us."

His gift of *perseverance* enables us to press through *disappointment*. At first this may appear next to impossible. There are times when the circumstances we face seem to directly oppose the promises He has made. Yet *He will give us the power to persevere.*

Abraham was promised that he would be the father of a nation. Yet his ability to procreate had long since expired. Joseph received a prophetic dream that he would be elevated to a place of influence—a vision of his brothers bowing down to him, acknowledging the work of the Lord in his life. Yet Joseph experienced his brothers' jealousy as they threw him into a pit, debating over selling him or killing him.

How did Abraham and Joseph hold onto God's promises in the face of overwhelming challenges?

My friend Lance Wallnau describes *perseverance* as the God-given ability to "endure the contradiction."

As you lift up God's promises in the face of contradicting circumstances, write your "Declaration of Perseverance."

CHAPTER 11

Face to Face

*The Lord will rescue me from
every evil attack and will bring me
safely to His heavenly kingdom.
To Him be glory for ever and ever
(2 Timothy 4:18).*

Almost six months after I had first stepped into the hospital, I was now walking out the front door, arm in arm with my wife. Leukemia was completely cleansed from my body. My ruptured appendix and all its poison were gone. Tubes that had been installed in my chest were now removed. My propensity to panic and to retain offenses was also being flushed from my system. His love was casting out my fears and cleansing me of my resentments.

I was healed! And I was being healed!

It would take a while for this to fully sink in. I certainly didn't feel like I could run a marathon. Even a brisk walk around the block would have done me in. But my heart was running and leaping and soaring. The brilliant sunshine of that morning felt like a warm embrace. It was a welcome change from the glaring fluorescent luminaries I had grown accustomed to. Around me the birds sang. I heard the noise of traffic once again and saw people scurrying to get to their next appointment. I was stepping back into a world I seemed to have forgotten.

As I stood by the passenger door, waiting for Sheri to unlock the car, I looked back at the hospital. I thought about the nursing staff, the doctors, the cleaning lady who talked with me daily about her grandchildren—people who tirelessly gave of themselves to make a difference in someone else's life. Often thanklessly.

As I stared at the building with its rows and rows of windows, I wondered about the people behind each pane of glass. What were their stories? Who was walking with them? Was anyone praying for them to find the door of hope in their dark valley? *As lights in the world, we must do a better job of reaching out to those who need Him!*

Then and there, I made a fresh resolve to renew my commitment to be an ambassador of hope. To represent Jesus to a world that desperately needs Him. To be so filled with His life that I would literally "re-present Him" to people, wherever I may be. To see His Kingdom come and witness His will being done, right here on the earth. *Just as it is in heaven.* These are far more than mere poetic words of what can become an empty ritual. They are Jesus' words. They are His mandate to us. He will honor them and fulfill them as we pray them and live them.

And that is why I tell you this story. To give you hope. So that you can give it away.

Hope is not a commodity or an emotion. It is a reality found in a Person. My greatest need was not to be healed. I needed the Healer. He healed my body. But even more, He healed my heart by drawing me close to His. Jesus truly is

Hope personified. He is worthy of all honor. And He is worthy of all our trust.

"Honey." I heard Sheri's voice. She was giving me one of those looks that said, "You're daydreaming again!"

I turned to see her face, illuminated in the bright May sunshine. She looked radiant. And tired.

"Let's go *home*, Mr. Hess," she said, ducking her head into the car.

As we drove down familiar roads toward our house, I felt like George Bailey running through the streets of Bedford Falls in the film *It's a Wonderful Life*, greeting the buildings of his hometown as if he were seeing them for the very first time.

Riding past our church building, I couldn't contain my emotions. I was so thankful for all our dear friends who believed and prayed. And then prayed some more. I was so grateful that they *believed*. They held onto Jesus' promises and trusted Him to be faithful.

Somewhere along the line, we have been lied to. We were told that God sends us sickness to teach us a lesson. At the same time, we were told that He doesn't do miracles anymore, that He somehow "got it out of His system" when Jesus walked the earth. In fact, this lie went so far as to say that if someone claims to have experienced a miracle, satan probably had something to do with it.

I pondered this for a moment.

God gives us diseases? And satan works miracles?

What a clever con!

This miracle we were experiencing was not a rare occurrence. In fact, what we call miracles, He calls normal. When Jesus said signs and wonders would follow those who believe Him, He did not use the word *occasionally*. And I was not getting special treatment simply because I was a pastor. He promises to give good gifts to *all* His children. He doesn't show partiality. He is not a shifty carnival worker who occasionally lets someone win in order to keep the rest of the customers at the counter. Though we have tried to change Him, He has not changed. He is still the God of miracles. He is still the One with whom nothing is impossible. *Nothing* is too hard for Him! We can trust Him. We can hope in Him. Not because we are gullible, but because He is *believable*!

A new door was opening wide for us. We had not uncovered a formula for healing. We had freshly discovered a Father who heals. A Father who wants to let the whole world know Him, as overwhelmingly as waves and currents move through the sea (see Hab. 2:14).

Jesus' example of how to pray was stirring us to new places in our trust in Him. He wants His Kingdom to come *here* on this planet. He longs for *His will* to be done here on the earth *just like it is in Heaven!* He was inspiring us to anticipate a heavenly invasion on planet Earth!

He was making it very clear that He still opens doors of hope in valleys of trouble! David said, "I would rather be a doorkeeper in the house of my God..." (Ps. 84:10a).

I asked the Lord to make me a doorkeeper, too.

At the door of hope.

As we pulled into the driveway, I took a fresh look at our house. Everything seemed just as it had been the day I left. The trees. The lawn. The porch posts taunting me to paint them. And Harry, our dog, stationed as a sentry on the back of the sofa, peering through the bay window, awaiting my return.

I was home at last!

I crawled into our bed to rest for a few moments before the children came home from school. It felt good to curl up in a familiar bed. No bed rails. No call buzzers. And no designer gowns! Because the children caught three separate buses at three separate times, they came home from school in 15-minute intervals. Although this schedule could be frustrating at times, today it would give me some focused moments with each one of them.

Bethany arrived first. Through droopy eyes, I took a good look at her. She was becoming quite a young woman, and I was so proud of her. She was a leader. She had a keen sense of right and wrong. Her eyes flashed at any hint of injustice.

I remembered a Christmas shopping trip we had taken a few months ago, during my first reprieve from hospital life. Chemo had taken my hair. All of it—even my eyelashes! Boy, did I miss them! Bethany wanted me to stay warm, so she said, "Let me buy you a new hat for that handsome head of yours!"

Standing with her in the mall beside a hat display filled with knitted caps, I felt like a human mannequin. Bethany must have tried every hat on the rack on my head, searching for just the right look as she giggled and fussed over me.

Two women came within earshot, staring at us with disdain. One said, loud enough for us to hear, "I think it's disgusting when older men shave their heads to pick up young women!"

Bethany's justice mode kicked in. With what little strength I had at the time, I restrained her, saving mall security from having to break up a major catfight.

This was my Bethany!

She smiled and asked me how I was feeling. Tears formed around her eyes as she gave me a big hug. "I knew you'd be all right," she whispered confidently in my ear.

Ben was the next one through the door.

Ben and I are the quieter ones in the family. It's not that we're shy. We just like to listen. This has worked well for us, since the other three in the family like to talk.

Of all the members of my family, Ben had concerned me the most during the past six months. He had grown up. He had risen to the occasion. We had never given him the "You're in charge now" speech. In fact, Sheri had worked hard to keep the family a family, despite my absence. But Ben had done his best to be the man of the house while I was away.

The other children had expressed themselves throughout the ordeal. Not just with words. They had openly shown their emotions.

Ben had not.

When he came through the front door, I heard his compassionate voice quietly say, "Is Dad home?"

"He's in the bedroom," I heard Sheri whisper. "He might be sleeping."

As he slowly peered around the door, our eyes met. In the next moment, he was plunging onto the bed, burying his face between my arm and chest. And then the dam burst. Convulsive weeping erupted from his heart. He held me tightly, as if he would never let go. From time to time, he would lift his head to look into my face. With swollen eyes, he would stare at me and simply say, "Dad!"

Brandon came home in the meantime. I heard Sheri's muffled voice talking to him inside the front door. I could not decipher her words, but I did not need to. I knew her well enough to know she had said something like, "Let's give Ben a little time with Dad." I could imagine Brandon nodding in agreement.

"I missed you, Ben. I really, really missed you," I blubbered, stroking his hair.

"Me, too," was all he could muster before letting more tears escape.

As I reflect on this moment, I think about the moments in life that test everything inside of us. Our pain tolerance. Our love. Our patience. Especially our capacity to trust and hope in God.

The question that gnaws at our sanity in these times is one that seems insatiable: *Why?*

Like incessant toddlers on a quest to drive their parents' patience over the brink, we ask, *Why? But why?*

The question is ultimately directed toward God, though we may not always address Him by name.

As I share my story, I realize that some may hear it and struggle. Though I tell it to encourage trust in a trustworthy God, I know that there are those who are disappointed with this same God. I was healed. Others have not been. Some have prayed just as earnestly, sincerely, and fervently as our friends prayed for me only to see their requests unmet and their hopes shattered. Again, the question: *Why?*

Solomon said, "Like one who takes away a garment on a cold day...is one who sings songs to a heavy heart" (Prov. 25:20). It is not my desire to burden hearts that are already heavy as I sing my song of praise.

The question "Why?" can open the door to necessary answers. Yet insatiable "Whys" can open the door to unbelief and close the door of hope.

I don't think we will have all of our "Why?" questions answered here on the earth. That's what Heaven is for. What we need more than an explanation to satisfy our intellect is His Presence to satisfy our souls.

We need Him.

He goes much deeper than thousands of words. He soothes us much better than hundreds of explanations ever could. Embracing Him fills, heals, and calms the deepest longings of our hearts.

King David wept bitterly after the death of his firstborn son. He spent days expressing his deepest grief. Then, he washed his face and fell into the arms of the Lord in worship. He didn't need a conference. He needed an encounter.

Here on my bed, Ben held me. He didn't need a scientific explanation of cancer and remission. He needed me. Just as we all need the Father.

With Ben lying beside me, Brandon bounded into the room. This robust nine-year-old was all eyes and ears. "Dad, you got healed!" he exclaimed, "and we're going to Disney World!" We all broke into laughter. It felt good to laugh again.

I felt alive.

And so...I did not die.

But I lived.

And now I am telling you what the Lord has done!

My Personal Journal of Hope

"The Lord is with me; He is my Helper. I will look in triumph on my enemies" (Ps. 118:7). When the psalmist penned these words, they were not expressed *after* the trial had passed. Instead, they were stated in faith-filled foresight before the end was in sight.

Ask your Father, who at this moment is boldly "declaring the end from the beginning" (Isa. 46:10) over your life, to fill you with His hope for your future. Join Him in His declaration.

Nothing takes the Lord by surprise. In fact, He sets His provision in place *before* the need arises. The boat was built *before* the Flood came. Jesus, the Lamb, was slain *before* the foundation of the world; the cross was in place *before* the curse.

And He opened the door of hope for you before you entered the valley of trouble!

How do you feel about Someone who is watching over you with such meticulous compassion?

CHAPTER 12

What the Lord Has Done

Return to your fortress, O prisoners
of hope; even now I announce that
I will restore twice as much to you
(Zechariah 9:12).

I am frequently asked the question: "What have you learned from this experience?" In the days immediately following my return home, I had very few answers to this inquiry. My mind had been so focused on living that I was often oblivious to what I was learning. All of my limited energy had been expended on standing and fighting and trusting and resting. Relieved to have the ordeal behind me, I was not so sure that I wanted to look back and see what I learned.

It took some time to readjust to home life. Months of hospital regimen had blurred my memory of normal household routines. A bed without side rails, meals at a table, pajamas that covered all the draft zones, and the ability to hug my family without tubes and masks getting in the way. All these things that I too often took for granted were now restored to me. And I treasured them.

Yet, in the years that have followed, I have become increasingly aware of some liberating revelations the Lord has taught me. One of the psalmists writes: "Great are the works of the Lord; they are pondered by all who delight in them" (Ps. 111:2). He did a mighty work in my life. The more I have pondered what He has done, the more my delight in Him has increased. Each time I reflect on these events, my heart is filled with renewed amazement at the faithfulness of God. Although I continue to learn something new each time I ponder, I'd like to pass on a few of the major lessons He has taught my heart.

1. **Every testimony can become *your testimony* about what the Lord has done.**

My passion is to do more than simply tell you *my* story. I want to literally *share* my story with you. It is now *your* story, too. I encourage you to receive this testimony and add it to your growing set of memories of God's goodness.

I have been stirred by David's words to the Lord:

> **Your testimonies** *have I taken* **as a heritage forever,** *for they are the rejoicing of my heart* (Psalm 119:111 NKJV).

David literally received as *his inheritance* the testimonies of all the Lord had ever done throughout the course of time. He literally made them his own. That's why he spoke of the parting of the Red Sea as if he had been standing right beside Moses when it happened (see Psalms 66 and 78). Even though he was separated from these events by hundreds of years, David claimed Moses' story as his own and declared it to a new generation, filling them with hope.

2. Something deadly happens when we forget what the Lord has done.

Psalm 78:9-11 describes a destructive chain of events that occurred when a well-armed battalion of skilled warriors failed to remember their history in God. Listen to their story:

The men of Ephraim, though armed with bows, **turned back** *on the day of battle; they* **did not keep God's covenant** *and* **refused to live by His law.** **They forgot** *what He had done, the wonders He had shown them* (Psalm 78:9-11).

These mighty warriors defeated themselves *on the day of battle* at the very hour for which they had trained. How did they defeat themselves?

They lost their courage when they needed it the most. On top of that, they fell into disobedience by neglecting to cultivate a devoted relationship with the Lord. What was the root of this tragedy?

They *forgot what the Lord had done,* ignoring the wonderful miracles He had worked among them. Wonders are events precipitated by the Lord that arrest your thoughts, filling your heart with awe. His wonders, great and small, are constantly occurring all around us.

Yet foreboding clouds of hopelessness often drift in, attempting to block them from our view. In a world abounding with cynical, critical, and complaining attitudes, miracles are often forgotten, overlooked, or explained away. His presence can be ignored. His works can be written off.

Despair thrives in this climate. Jesus warns us of a time when "men will faint from terror" (Luke 21:26). There will be people who live "without hope and without God in the world" (Eph. 2:12). Why?

They forget what He has done, ignoring the wonders He has shown them.

3. **In direct contrast, powerful things happen when we remember and talk about His miraculous interventions in human lives.**

Jesus said that we would overcome the devil himself by the power of His blood and by the very word of our testimony (see Rev. 12:11)! As you receive my story, I encourage you to add it to your collection of the wonders He has done. Make it part of *your* word of testimony. Tell people what He has done in your life and the lives of others throughout history. Testimonies are part of your supernatural arsenal. Naturally interject His stories into your daily conversations. By doing so, you will change the climate. Try this sometime today: Instead of engaging in the usual conversational fodder about the weather, the economy, the government, or endless lists of complaints, talk about something the Lord has done. Not in a smugly religious way. Just naturally talk about something that the naturally supernatural One has accomplished. Then watch what happens! Notice the climate change. Stories of hope create an atmosphere of expectation. If Jesus did it before, He can do it again! Your act of sharing may very well open the door for you to pray for someone right there in that moment—because stories of His faithfulness stir up hope.

Mark tells the story of Jesus setting a man free from thousands of demons. He was said to have a legion of them, a Roman military term for over 6,000 soldiers. Imagine being tormented by that many evil spirits!

This man lived in the region of the Gerasenes, among the tombstones of the local graveyard. He was known to run around naked, cutting himself and piercing the night air with his blood-curdling screams. He shattered the nerves of the residents of that region. He also significantly lowered their property value!

With a voice of authority, Jesus evicted the demons from this man. With a heart of love, He healed and restored him. Grateful to be set free, this man, now "dressed and in his right mind" (Mark 5:15), asked Jesus if he could travel with Him as one of His disciples. Amazingly, Jesus denied his request. Instead He instructed the man, "Go home to your family and tell them how much the Lord has done for you, and how He has had mercy on you" (Mark 5:19).

And he did just that.

But his story did not just stop there. Instead, this man went throughout the Decapolis, a ten-city region in Syria, simply telling his story. It spread like wildfire. He didn't compile a ten-week series on deliverance. He simply shared a two-minute story of hope. And his simple story opened doors of hope for people all over that part of the world.

Jesus' first trip to the Decapolis territory was met with strong resistance. In fact, the people begged Him to leave their region (see Mark 5:17). But as this man's story spread, an atmosphere of expectancy erupted. When Jesus returned to the Decapolis territory a short while later, they brought sick people to Him, expecting them to be healed. The climate had changed. They were "overwhelmed with amazement" and "kept talking about" all that Jesus had done among them (Mark 7:36-37).

A ten-city region was transformed; all because one man told His story.

There is a famine for hope in this world. Together, we can eradicate hopelessness in the name of Jesus, the Hope of Glory (see Col. 1:27)!

4. Hope is contagious.

Unlike our cultural use of the word *hope*, it is not biblically defined as "wishful thinking" ("I *hope* it doesn't rain tomorrow!"). It is not crossing our fingers in dreaded anticipation of what may or may not happen. Instead, the word *hope*, as it is used in the New Testament, means "joyful and confident expectation."[1] In the center of the deepest valley of trouble, hope abides (it continues to be present; it lasts, endures, and survives[2]). Faith abides, too. And, most powerfully of all, His love abides (see 1 Cor. 13:13). We can ceaselessly hope in a God who endlessly loves us! This hope He gives "does not disappoint us, because God has poured out His love into our hearts by the Holy Spirit, whom He has given us" (Rom. 5:5).

Throughout the six-month fight for my life, His gift of hope was my constant companion. Even in my most despondent days, His encouragement pierced through the storm clouds like brilliant shafts of relentless sunlight.

We were not made to live without hope!

Solomon warns: "Hope deferred makes the heart sick" (Prov. 13:12). He did not say, "Answers delayed make the heart sick." Nor did he say, "If God doesn't respond to your prayers in a reasonable amount of time, you will self-destruct." Instead, he advises us: "The moment you *stop hoping* is the moment your heart becomes sick — weak, overwhelmed with debilitating grief."[3]

We were never made to live without hope.

At the moment you are reading these words, you may be overwhelmed (as I was) by your circumstances. You've roamed the dark valley of trouble and perhaps feel like you cannot find the door of hope. Run into the presence of the One who welcomes us to cast all our cares upon Him. In drawing near to Jesus, we find a true companion, One who was tested in every way that we are, yet remained sinless.

Above everything else, we need Him!

David, in one of his many troubled times, talked to himself. He said:

> *Why are you downcast, O my soul? Why so disturbed within me?* **Put your hope in God,** *for I will yet praise Him, my Savior and my God* (Psalm 42:5-6a).

He refused to passively accept hopelessness as the home for his soul. Instead, he stood up in his troubled valley and pursued the door of hope. And he found it! He put his confident expectations in God and was not disappointed.

We will find ourselves baffled by life at times. The apostle Paul was. He said there were moments when he was "perplexed" (2 Cor. 4:8 KJV). He used this word to describe a state in which you are "lacking resources, not knowing which way to turn."[4] Ever been there?

Yet Paul went on to say that despite these moments of great uncertainty, he was "not in despair" (2 Cor. 4:8). He never found himself in the place where he had to "renounce all hope," being "utterly destitute of all resources."[5] We may lack understanding, but we do not have to lose hope. Only Jesus can give us this hope beyond reason.

My prayer for you today is this:

> *May* **the God of all hope** *fill you with all joy and peace as you trust in Him, so that you may* **overflow with hope** *by the power of the Holy Spirit* (Romans 15:13).

He still opens doors of hope in valleys of trouble.

And right now, He's holding the door open for you!

ENDNOTES

1. Thayer's Greek Definitions.
2. Ibid.
3. Brown-Driver-Briggs' Hebrew Definitions.
4. Thayer's Greek Definitions.
5. Ibid.

My Personal Journal of Hope

Hope is contagious. As we receive testimonies of God's faithfulness in the lives of others, hope is ignited in our hearts as well.

David said, "Your testimonies I have taken as a heritage forever" (Ps. 119:111a NKJV). He received the stories of God's miraculous interventions throughout the generations and made them his own. He wrote songs about them. He reminded his people of *their* "history of hope." He did this in spite of the fact that many of these events happened years before he was even born!

The result? David said, "[These testimonies] are the rejoicing of my heart" (Ps. 119:111b NKJV).

What is your "history of hope?" What stories of His faithfulness have you cherished through the years?

There is a famine of hope in the land. Far too many people live "without hope and without God in the world" (Eph. 2:12).

How do you feel about this? How can you serve as an ambassador of hope to other people—even while you are still walking through your own valley of trouble?

CHAPTER 13

Signs and Wonders

*Most assuredly, I say to you, he who believes
in Me, the works that I do he will
do also; and greater works than these
he will do, because I go to My Father*
(John 14:12 NKJV).

This door of hope did not just swing open for me. It swung wide open for our church and other churches in our region.

Since the day I was healed, we have seen increasing numbers of people touched by the presence and power of the Lord Jesus. Blind eyes have been restored. Deaf ears have been opened. Tumors have disappeared. Diseases have left bodies. And most of all, people's hearts are being reconciled to the heart of the Lord.

We have seen children, battling severe infirmities while still in the womb, amazingly healed by the Lord prior to their births. One little girl had a rare bone malady that caused her entire intestinal area to become filled with bone marrow. Her parents were informed that she would probably not survive the birth process. Even if she did, she would only live a few moments without an excretory system. Declining the doctor's recommendation of an abortion, we prayed. Within the womb, a creative miracle took place. The before and after X-rays undeniably attest to the amazing work the Lord did in this growing, healthy little girl.

Another mother was told to abort her son due to multiple tests verifying that he would be extremely mentally handicapped. Refusing to end his life, she prayed. Others stood with her. During a prayer session, one of our members received an impression from the Lord that this boy was healed in the womb. Several months later, the word was confirmed as her healthy son was born into the world.

Such miracles have not been limited to church services. Shopping malls. Factories. Classrooms. Offices. Sports fields. The kitchen table. These have all become natural ministry settings.

Nor have these wonders occurred only when leaders or seasoned older believers pray. Young and old alike have participated in opening these doors of hope. While shopping with her mother, a six-year-old girl said, "Mommy, we must pray for that woman over there," pointing to an older lady in the store. The mother, attempting to discourage a public scene, replied, "We'll pray for her when we get to the car."

"No, Mommy," she insisted. "Jesus wants us to pray for her now."

Apparently overhearing the discussion, the woman smiled at them. Stirred by her daughter's boldness, the mother explained, "My daughter would like to pray for you."

With love-filled boldness, this little girl said, "Jesus told me that even though you are smiling outside, you are sad inside. He wants to make you happy again."

The woman's lower lip began to quiver. Through tears she said, "My husband died a year ago, and I never cried. I tried to be strong for everyone else." This simple prayer of a six-year-old opened a door of healing for a grieving widow.

One evening as we were praying for people at the close of a service, I was sitting on the front row watching people of all ages pray for people with all kinds of needs. A four-year-old girl stood beside me, and I smiled at her.

"Do you want to pray for someone?" I asked.

She nodded and pointed to a woman who was receiving prayer.

I escorted her to join a group of people who were already praying for the woman.

"Did Jesus tell you where she hurts?" I asked.

Nodding once again, she pointed toward the woman's lower back on the right side. Her small arm could barely reach that spot as she extended her hand to pray. The moment this little girl's hand touched the woman's back, the woman said, "Something very hot is touching my right kidney!"

The little girl prayed for just a moment, then scurried along to play with some of her friends. Several days later we learned this woman was battling cancer in her right kidney. She had just had an X-ray that morning to verify it. Certain she was healed that evening, she returned to the doctor's office the next day. Because of insurance regulations, she paid for a second X-ray out of her own pocket. The results? Not only had cancer been completely cleansed from her kidney, she also had pre-cancerous nodules cleansed from her lymph nodes!

Our church's food ministry has experienced a supernatural overhaul. Now people are receiving signs and wonders along with their bread and milk. Miraculous doors have repeatedly opened for people to get jobs, get saved, and get healed. One day 12 men turned their hearts over to Jesus while being prayed for in the streets. A legally-blind woman's eyesight was completely restored. In celebration, she read a Bible aloud to everyone, without the need for her thick, prescription glasses. A Muslim man, barely able to walk due to a hip injury, was amazingly healed within moments. Dancing and twirling while holding his cane over his head, he exclaimed, "Jesus Christ answers prayer!" In fact, he was so elated that he forgot to take his groceries along with him as he strutted down the sidewalk toward his home.

Sometimes doors of hope swing open with a dramatic rush. Cancers leave. Tumors disappear. Eyes and ears are opened.

Other times, with a simple word and a simple prayer, years of bondage are broken. Prodigals come home to the Father. Sad hearts receive joy. Fractured relationships are mended. And His Kingdom comes.

I close my story with another example that challenged me to walk with Jesus in a new way. Miracles are called signs and wonders throughout the New Testament. They are wonders because they overwhelm our senses as we wonder how Jesus accomplished them. They are signs because they point to something greater than the miracle itself.

This particular wonder took place in the life of one of our church's young men, Benjamin, who had been born pigeon-toed. His severely twisted feet had always made walking a challenge. Now at age 13, his physically frustrating condition would cause him to fall flat on his face several times each day. It was emotionally devastating as others would laugh at him, giving him the name "Pigeon" as his new identity.

One evening, in an atmosphere of corporate prayer, Benjamin felt intense heat coursing through his feet and ankles. What happened in the next few moments was even more astonishing. As if supernatural hands were gripping his feet, Benjamin said, "I could feel my feet being pushed out."

Dumbfounded, he stared at his feet. They were new feet!

He ran up to me and said, "Look at my feet. I'm not pigeon-toed anymore! I can walk. I can run."

With that, Benjamin began running back and forth in the front of the church. A small crowd gathered to cheer him on. When he finished his victory lap, he looked at us and said, "I used to walk like this." At that moment, he struggled with all his might to twist his feet back into their former position. But he couldn't because they were healed.

Puzzled, he looked at me and said, "I can't walk like I used to walk!"

The wonder was the miracle that Jesus worked in his feet.

The sign was the statement that came out of his mouth.

We were created to live like this. We were born to *follow Jesus*, with signs of His power and love *following us*. This is how Jesus lived. This is *normal* Christianity. If we wonder what the will of God is, all we have to do is look at Jesus. He is the "Word" of God Who "became flesh" (John 1:14). He is the will of God personified.

My appetite to know Jesus and walk His supernatural ways started early. As a young boy, I would awaken quickly on a Saturday morning and dash to our black-and-white television set in the living room. The "Cisco Kid," along with "Roy Rogers" and "Sky King," were waiting for me. Wearing my cowboy hat and boots while riding my plastic hobby horse, I weekly enforced justice with the best of the West.

Then one week, I met another television friend who captured my heart. Her name was Kathryn Kuhlman. Her melodic voice and glowing smile held my attention. Sitting cross-legged on the floor, I eagerly awaited her entrance onto the television screen. With graceful movements in her flowing gown, she would always inquire, "Have you been waiting for me?" Nodding my head, I told her every time that I was. Week after week I was hungry to hear about miracles Jesus was doing. Kathryn convinced me that nothing was too hard for Jesus to do. We could expect miracles to happen every day. She planted good seeds in my young heart. These seeds are still growing in me today.

In the words of young Benjamin, "I can't walk like I used to walk!" And I don't want to go back. I will not return to the days of being a safe and silent Christian. I have crossed a threshold where Jesus' supernatural ministry has become natural. Where miracles are normal. Where risks can be taken without fear, because His love makes us fearless. Oh, there are still valleys of trouble. Not every situation we pray for turns out like these few stories I've shared. But I have seen more miracles in the last several years than I have ever seen in my life. And we are going after more!

There are doors of hope just waiting for you to enter. There are windows in Heaven that your faith and obedience will open. So I appeal to you to join the growing international community of lovers and followers of Jesus Christ who believe Him, who move with Him.

And who confidently hope in Him.

A Final Word

A few years have passed since I lived the story contained in these pages. What full years they have been!

Rosemary retired shortly after I left the hospital. We kept in touch by phone and letters mostly. Once in a while she would stop by the church to see me during the afternoon. We sat in the lobby and talked and laughed together. The weather. Our families. The political scene. You name it. We talked about it.

It was on one of those afternoons that she gave her heart to Jesus Christ. As simple and sincere as you please. We cried a lot that day, and we sang a little. It was a moment I had prayed for.

A short time later, I received a call from Rosemary's daughter asking me to oversee her mother's funeral. "Mom went to Heaven during the night. She just slipped away in her sleep," she told me as I let the tears flow freely. We honored her life on a cold February afternoon in the middle of a snowstorm.

Rosemary hated snow. And she hated it when people made a fuss over her.

But she got both that day.

In the spring of 2006, I walked my daughter down the aisle at her wedding. The church was filled with family and friends. My mind was packed with a whirlwind of memories. *How these years had sailed by! My little girl! My pacifier-sucking, blanket-holding, piggy-back-riding baby had grown up! Here she was, looking like she stepped off the page of a bridal magazine.* I swallowed hard, gave her my arm, and we started our march to the sanctuary with an army of bridesmaids following us like ducks swishing to the pond.

For a moment, I recalled that terrifying night a few years before when I had one of my fiercest battles with despair. I was haunted by images of Bethany walking down the aisle at her wedding—alone. Torrents of anxious thoughts had assaulted me. Hopeless lies from the father of lies had tried to rob me of all hope.

Yet here we were. Walking down the aisle. Together.

The wedding pictures captured a slight grin on my face as I escorted Bethany that day. You might ask, "What were you thinking at that moment?" The phrase: "Liar, liar, pants on fire!" had run through my mind a few times.

I am so grateful to have experienced so much life in these years. They are days I will never take for granted. People often say, "If I had experienced half the miracles you experienced, I'd be grateful, too." Although my physical healing is an important part of my testimony, it is not the most important part.

I am truly amazed that my sins have been forgiven.

Jesus healed my body, but most of all He freed my soul. Miracles alone won't change us. The transformation comes when we receive His amazing grace.

As I write these final words, I want to invite you to make the most important choice you could ever make. Surrender your life to Jesus Christ. Ask Him to forgive you. Ask Him to fill you with His love and His power, transforming your whole being. Your words can be as simple as this:

> Jesus, thank You for coming after me. Thank You for dying in my place and suffering my penalty for the crimes I committed against You!

> Jesus, I need You! I ask You to forgive me for all of my sins. I surrender my life to You. I yield my will to Your will. Help me to follow You all of my days.

> I am no longer in charge of my life. You are! Please fill me with Your Holy Spirit and empower me to walk in Your ways.

> *I thank You for hearing the cry of my heart.*

> *I trust You, Jesus.*

> *In Your name, Amen* (So be it!).

Author Contact Information

CHRIST COMMUNITY CHURCH

1201 Slate Hill Road
Camp Hill, PA 17011

Website: www.christcc.org

- ❖ Podcasts of sermons are available (free of charge) on the Website.
- ❖ CDs of sermons, conferences, etc. are also available via the Website.
- ❖ Prayer requests and testimonies can also be sent to us via the Website.